Cracking the Chakra Code:

Unlock the Secrets of Energy and Personal Transformation

A Practical Path to Healing, Growth, and
Empowerment Through Chakra Balancing

D. Kashuba

Table of Contents

Introduction

Let me start with a little story from my own life. A few years ago, I found myself completely drained. I was juggling a demanding job, family responsibilities, and trying to maintain some semblance of a social life. One day, I woke up and felt like a zombie. No amount of coffee could shake the exhaustion. That's when a friend suggested I try energy healing. I was skeptical. But I was also desperate. So, I decided to give it a shot. Little did I know that decision would change my life forever.

I walked into my first session, trying to figure out what to expect. The healer spoke about chakras—these mysterious energy centers in our bodies that I'd only ever heard of in passing. As the session progressed, I felt an almost magical shift. My mind cleared, my body relaxed, and I felt alive for the first time in months. That experience sparked a journey of discovery and healing that has led me here, writing this book for you.

So, what are chakras, and why should you care? Chakras are energy centers in our bodies that regulate various physical, emotional, and spiritual functions. Think of them as spinning wheels of energy that need to be balanced for us to feel our best. When our chakras are out of balance, we might feel stressed, anxious, or physically ill. But when they are in harmony, we experience a sense of well-being and vitality.

The purpose of this book is simple: to help you unlock, discover, and release your inner energy. Whether you're new to the concept of chakras or have been exploring energy healing for years, this book aims to provide practical, easy-to-follow guidance. You'll find step-by-step instructions, quick references, and interactive elements like QR codes that link to guided or video tutorials. I aim to make understanding and working with your chakras as accessible and enjoyable as possible.

This book is for everyone. Whether you're a busy professional, a devoted parent, a curious young adult, or someone simply seeking a deeper connection with yourself, this book has something for you. You don't need any prior knowledge or special skills. All you need is an open mind and a willingness to explore.

As you read, you can expect to gain a clear understanding of what chakras are and how they affect your life. You'll learn practical techniques to balance your energy centers and improve your overall well-being. Each chapter will focus on a different chakra, providing detailed insights and actionable steps. And don't worry—I've sprinkled in a bit of humor and personal anecdotes to keep things light and engaging.

Now, a bit about me. My name is Dawn, and I am passionate about helping people overcome energy imbalances and achieve holistic wellness. I've spent years studying various forms of energy healing and have seen firsthand how transformative this work can be. My mission is to share this knowledge in a way that is both reputable and easy to follow. I've poured my heart and soul into this book and am excited to share it with you.

This isn't just another book on chakras. It's an interactive experience designed to guide you on a journey of self-discovery and healing. With practical applications, clear guidance, and a kindhearted tone, I hope this book becomes a valuable resource for you. So grab a comfy seat, maybe a cup of tea, and let's dive in.

I want you to feel inspired and motivated as you turn each page. This book is an invitation to explore a deeper part of yourself, to find balance, and to live with more joy and vitality. The journey might sometimes challenge you, but I promise it will also be incredibly rewarding.

So here we are, at the start of something extraordinary. Are you ready to unlock the power within you? Let's get started.

Chapter 1:
Understanding the Basics of Chakras

A few years ago, I stared blankly at my laptop screen in a coffee shop's cozy corner. My mind was a whirlwind of grocery lists, upcoming deadlines, and a nagging thought about whether I'd remembered to lock the front door that morning. I could have been lost in thought anywhere—a long drive, waiting in line at the grocery store, or even absentmindedly flipping through TV channels late at night. My body was present, but my thoughts were constantly somewhere else.

As I sat there, sipping my coffee, I overheard a nearby conversation about chakras. At first, I dismissed it, thinking, "Great, another mystical concept I'll never understand." But something about the way they spoke caught my attention. I couldn't resist and asked them, "I've heard about chakras before, but I've never really understood what they are. Could you explain it to me?"

To my surprise, they warmly welcomed me into their conversation. What they shared wasn't full of confusing spiritual jargon but was explained with simplicity and clarity. They likened chakras to tuning an instrument, describing how these energy centers needed to be balanced for us to feel genuinely aligned. They discussed how energy could become blocked, affecting your emotions and physical well-being.

As they spoke, something clicked. Maybe this wasn't just some mystical theory but the key to understanding why I often felt out of sync, even when everything seemed fine. That moment was the spark that led me on an unexpected deep dive into the world of chakras and energy. It opened the door to self-discovery, helping me learn how to balance and channel my energy in ways that completely transformed my outlook and well-being. Now, I'm excited to share what I've learned with you, and I hope this journey can help you find the same sense of clarity and balance.

What Are Chakras? A Beginner's Guide

Let's start with the basics. The word "chakra" comes from Sanskrit, meaning "wheel" or "disk." Imagine these as spinning wheels of energy located along your spine, each playing a vital role in your physical, emotional, and spiritual health. Chakras are not something you can see or touch, but their effects can be felt in various aspects of your life. Think of them as the body's energy hubs, regulating everything from your basic survival instincts to your deepest spiritual connections.

There are seven major chakras, each with its own unique characteristics and functions. The Root Chakra (Muladhara) is located at the base of your spine. This chakra is all about grounding and stability, like the roots of a tree. Next is the Sacral Chakra (Svadhisthana) in your lower abdomen. This one governs your creativity, sexuality, and pleasure. Moving up, we have the Solar Plexus Chakra (Manipura) in your upper abdomen. It's the powerhouse that fuels your confidence and personal power.

Then there's the Heart Chakra (Anahata), located in the center of your chest. It's the epicenter of love, compassion, and emotional balance. The Throat Chakra (Vishuddha) is next, positioned at your throat. This chakra is all about communication and self-expression. The Third Eye Chakra (Ajna) is still higher and located between your eyebrows. It's the seat of intuition and inner wisdom. Finally, we reach the Crown Chakra (Sahasrara) above your head. This chakra connects you to higher consciousness and spiritual enlightenment.

So, why do chakras matter? When your chakras are balanced, you feel good—physically, emotionally, and spiritually. Balanced chakras mean your energy flows freely, promoting overall well-being. However, when chakras are blocked or out of sync, you might experience various issues, from physical ailments to emotional turbulence. For instance, an imbalanced

Root Chakra might make you feel anxious or insecure, while a blocked Throat Chakra could result in communication problems.

There are some common misconceptions about chakras that we need to clear up. First off, chakras are not tied to any specific religion. While they originate from ancient Indian texts and are significant in Hinduism and Buddhism, you don't need to adhere to any particular faith to benefit from chakra work. Chakras are about energy, something we all have, regardless of our spiritual beliefs.

Another point of confusion is the difference between chakras and other energy systems like meridians, which are used in traditional Chinese medicine. While both systems deal with energy flow, they are distinct in their structure and approach. Meridians are like energy highways, whereas chakras are energy hubs. Understanding this distinction can help you appreciate the unique benefits that chakra healing offers.

So, as we delve deeper into this fascinating subject, keep an open mind and a curious heart. Chakras might seem mystical initially, but as you begin to work with them, you'll find that they offer practical, tangible benefits. Whether you're looking to boost your energy, improve your emotional health, or deepen your spiritual connection, chakras can be a powerful tool in your wellness toolkit. Let's explore this together, one chakra at a time, and discover how these energy centers can transform your life.

The Seven Energy Centers: Locations and Functions

Imagine standing on the ground, feeling the earth beneath your feet, steady and unyielding. This is your Root Chakra (Muladhara), located at the base of your spine. It's your foundation, your anchor, providing stability and security. When balanced, you feel grounded and safe, like nothing can shake you. Physically, it connects to your legs, feet, and bones—anything that touches the earth. Emotionally, it's tied to your basic survival instincts, like food, shelter, and safety. You might feel anxious or insecure when out of balance, like the ground is shifting beneath you.

Moving upward, we arrive at the Sacral Chakra (Svadhisthana) in the lower abdomen, about two inches below the navel. Picture this as a swirling pool of creative energy. It governs your emotions, desires, and sexuality. When it's in harmony, you feel a surge of creativity and pleasure in your activities. This chakra ties into your reproductive organs and is crucial for nurturing relationships and creative endeavors. Imbalances here might manifest as emotional instability or a lack of creative inspiration, leaving you stuck or unfulfilled.

Next, we encounter the Solar Plexus Chakra (Manipura) in the upper abdomen around the stomach area. Think of this as your inner sun, radiating power, confidence, and control. It's your powerhouse, giving you the self-esteem to take on challenges. Physically, it connects to your digestive system. When balanced, you feel confident and in control of your life. Out of balance, it can lead to digestive issues and feelings of powerlessness or low self-esteem, making it hard to assert yourself or make decisions.

In the center of your chest lies the Heart Chakra (Anahata), the bridge between the lower and upper chakras. This is your emotional epicenter, responsible for love, compassion, and emotional balance. Open and balanced allow you to experience deep connections with others and genuine self-love. Physically, it's linked to the heart and lungs. If this chakra is blocked, you might feel emotionally numb or find it challenging to form meaningful relationships. It's like having a wall around your heart, keeping love out and your true feelings in.

The Throat Chakra (Vishuddha) is situated in the throat area and is your communication hub. It's all about expressing your truth, speaking clearly, and listening effectively. When balanced, you can easily articulate your thoughts and feelings. This chakra is tied to the throat, neck, and vocal cords.

If imbalanced, you might struggle with communication or feel like your voice isn't being heard. You might even experience physical symptoms like a sore throat or thyroid issues.

Next, we have the Third Eye Chakra (Ajna) between your eyebrows. This is your seat of intuition, insight, and clarity. Think of it as your internal GPS, guiding you through life with inner wisdom. Physically, it's connected to the brain, eyes, and forehead. A balanced Third Eye Chakra enhances your intuition and mental clarity. When it's blocked, you might feel disconnected from your inner voice or struggle with decision-making, like navigating through fog without a map.

Finally, we reach the Crown Chakra (Sahasrara), positioned at the top of the head. This chakra connects you to the divine, promoting spiritual enlightenment and unity with the universe. Physically, it's linked to the brain and nervous system. When balanced, you feel a profound sense of peace and connection to something greater than yourself. If blocked, you might feel spiritually disconnected or experience a lack of purpose.

Each chakra pulses with life and is pivotal in maintaining your overall health. Envision your energy flowing seamlessly across all chakras—this harmony fosters a sanctuary for your mental, physical, and emotional well-being, igniting a sense of joy and vitality within. Becoming adept at noticing the subtlest signs of disharmony enables you to adjust these vital energy centers before they adversely affect your health. Living in tune with your chakras means understanding their positions and functions deeply and acknowledging how they shape both your physical state and your emotional experiences. This knowledge is your gateway to a life of balance and richness, allowing each chakra to operate in perfect harmony and support a state of radiant health.

Visual Aids and Diagrams

Imagine for a moment you're looking at a beautiful, intricate map. Each landmark is clearly marked, helping you navigate through unfamiliar territory. Visual aids and diagrams serve a similar purpose in understanding chakras. They clearly represent where each chakra is along your spine, making grasping their positions and interconnectedness easier. Picture a diagram showing the seven chakras as colorful, spinning wheels aligned from the base of your spine to the top of your head. Each chakra is represented by a different color: red for the Root Chakra, orange for the Sacral Chakra, yellow for the Solar Plexus Chakra, green for the Heart Chakra, blue for the Throat Chakra, indigo for the Third Eye Chakra, and violet for the Crown Chakra. These colors aren't just for aesthetic appeal; they have specific vibrational frequencies that resonate with each chakra, aiding their balance and healing.

Color-coded illustrations can be incredibly helpful, especially for visual learners. They offer a quick reference that makes it easy to remember which chakra is associated with which area of your body and its corresponding color. For example, seeing a green heart in the center of the chest instantly reminds you of the Heart Chakra and its role in love and compassion. Visual aids can also show how energy flows between chakras, emphasizing their interconnectedness. Just like a river that feeds into various lakes and streams, the energy in your body flows through these chakras, affecting everything from your physical health to your emotional well-being.

Now, let's talk about the interconnectedness of chakras. Think of your chakras as a team of players in a symphony. Each has a unique role but must work harmoniously to create beautiful music. When one chakra is out of balance, it can throw the entire system off, much like a discordant note in a melody. For instance, if your Root Chakra is blocked, you might feel anxious and insecure, which can affect your creativity and pleasure, governed by the Sacral Chakra. This imbalance can ripple up to your Solar Plexus Chakra, undermining your confidence and personal power.

Maintaining balance across all chakras is crucial for overall well-being. It's not enough to focus on just one or two chakras; you need to ensure that energy flows freely through all of them. This holistic approach can help you achieve a state of equilibrium where you feel grounded, creative, confident, loving, expressive, intuitive, and spiritually connected. Picture it like tuning a guitar. If one string is off-key, the whole instrument sounds out of tune. But the music flows effortlessly when each string is perfectly tuned, creating harmony.

Visualization Exercise

To help you visualize this interconnectedness, consider a simple exercise. Close your eyes and imagine a warm, glowing ball of energy at the base of your spine. As you take deep breaths, visualize this energy moving upward, passing through each chakra and lighting it up in its respective color. Feel the energy flow smoothly from the Root Chakra through the Sacral, Solar Plexus, Heart, Throat, Third Eye, and finally to the Crown Chakra. This visualization can help you sense the energy flow and identify areas where it might be blocked or sluggish.

Incorporating these visual aids and exercises into your daily practice can significantly affect how you understand and work with your chakras. They offer a tangible way to see and feel the energy centers within your body, making the abstract concept of chakras more concrete and accessible. Therefore, when you meditate or engage in yoga, let these visual guides illuminate your path. They're more than mere images; they're tools to steer you through the complex terrain of your inner energy, ensuring every chakra is in harmonious balance.

Understanding the Chakra Locations and QR Code

The image provided shows a woman in a yoga meditation pose with seven symbols placed along her body. These symbols represent the seven main chakras, which are energy centers that run from the base of the spine to the crown of the head. Each chakra is associated with specific body areas and influences physical, emotional, and spiritual well-being.

- **Crown Chakra**: Located at the top of the head.

- **Third Eye Chakra**: Positioned between the eyebrows.

- **Throat Chakra**: Located at the throat.

- **Heart Chakra**: In the center of the chest.

- **Solar Plexus Chakra**: Just above the navel.

- **Sacral Chakra**: Below the navel.

- **Root Chakra**: At the base of the spine.

To help you better visualize the exact locations of these chakras, scan the QR code below. The code will take you to a short video that provides a visual guide to the chakra placements on the body. Simply scan the code using your smartphone's camera, and you'll be taken directly to the video.

Of course, you'll likely have to skip an ad first—because who doesn't love a good ad before a chakra alignment video? But once you're past that, the video will help you understand where each chakra is located and how they align along the spine, from the root to the crown.

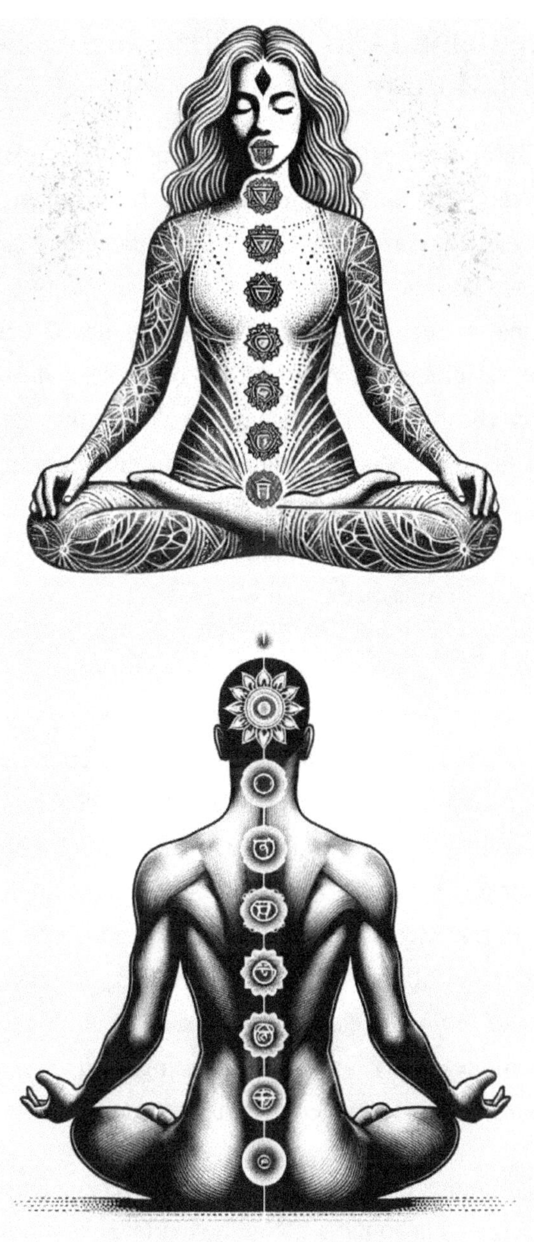

The Science Behind Chakras: Bridging Ancient Wisdom and Modern Research

The concept of chakras is rooted in ancient Indian texts dating back thousands of years. The earliest mentions can be found in the Vedas and Upanishads, where chakras are described as vital energy centers within the body. These texts laid the groundwork for understanding how the flow of energy—or prana—affects our physical and spiritual well-being. Over time, this knowledge was integrated into practices like yoga and Ayurveda. Yoga, with its asanas (postures) and pranayama (breathing techniques), was designed to balance these energy centers, promoting harmony between the mind and body. Ayurveda, the ancient system of medicine, used herbs, diet, and other natural remedies to maintain this balance, highlighting the interconnectedness of all aspects of life.

Fast forward to today, and you'll find that modern science is beginning to catch up with what ancient sages knew. Researchers in the field of bioenergetic medicine study the body's electromagnetic field and how it influences our health. These studies suggest that chakras correspond to nerve plexuses and endocrine glands, which are crucial for bodily functions. The body's electromagnetic field, measured through technologies like EEG and EKG, shows that our bodies are indeed energetic systems. Studies on meditation and mindfulness further support this, illustrating how these practices can alter brain waves, reduce stress, and improve overall health. When you meditate, you're not just calming your mind; you're also influencing your body's energy centers, promoting healing and balance.

The mind-body connection is another area where science and ancient wisdom intersect. Psychosomatic medicine explores how our emotions and mental states can manifest as physical symptoms. Stress, for instance, can lead to digestive issues, headaches, and even chronic illnesses. This is where chakras come into play. When stressed, your energy flow is disrupted, leading to imbalances in specific chakras. For example, anxiety might affect your Root Chakra, making you feel ungrounded and insecure. By addressing these imbalances through techniques like meditation, you can restore the natural flow of energy, alleviating emotional and physical symptoms.

Modern applications of chakra knowledge are vast and varied. In holistic health practices, chakras are often the focal point. Reiki, a form of energy healing, involves channeling energy through the practitioner's hands to the patient's chakras, promoting balance and healing. Acupuncture, rooted in traditional Chinese medicine, targets meridians, energy pathways similar to chakras. Both practices aim to restore the body's natural energy flow, highlighting the universality of these concepts across different cultures. In psychotherapy, techniques like guided imagery and mindfulness are used to help patients connect with their inner selves, addressing emotional blockages that might be linked to chakra imbalances.

One fascinating example is the integration of chakra work into counseling. Therapists trained in energy psychology might use techniques like Emotional Freedom Techniques (EFT), which involve tapping specific points on the body while focusing on emotional issues. This method aims to balance the body's energy system, providing relief from anxiety, trauma, and other emotional disturbances. By combining traditional talk therapy with energy work, therapists can offer a more holistic approach to healing.

In the end, the science behind chakras is as much about modern research as it is about ancient wisdom. While the scientific community continues to explore and validate these concepts, the practical benefits are undeniable. Whether practicing yoga, meditating, or seeking holistic therapies, understanding your chakras can provide a new dimension to your well-being. This blend of ancient and modern insights offers a comprehensive framework for living a balanced, healthy life.

The Mind-Body Connection: How Chakras Influence Physical Health

Have you ever noticed how stress settles in your back or how excitement can make your stomach churn? That's not just coincidence; it's your chakras at work. Take the **Root Chakra**, for instance. Located at the base of your spine, it's crucial for bone health and lower body stability. When balanced, you feel grounded and secure, like a tree with deep roots. But when it's out of whack, you might experience lower back pain, leg issues, or even bone density problems. Have you ever had a day where you felt completely unsteady? Your Root Chakra might be crying out for help.

Next up is the **Sacral Chakra**, nestled in your lower abdomen, just below the navel. This is the home of your reproductive health and urinary system. Think of it as the wellspring of your creativity and passion. When balanced, your reproductive organs function smoothly, and you feel a healthy desire and pleasure. However, an imbalanced Sacral Chakra can lead to issues like urinary tract infections or reproductive problems. Have you ever felt creatively blocked or emotionally bogged down? Your Sacral Chakra might need some TLC.

Now, consider the **Solar Plexus Chakra**, located in your upper abdomen. This one is all about your digestive health and metabolism. Imagine it as the furnace that fuels your body, transforming food into energy. When it's in harmony, your digestion is smooth, and your metabolism hums along nicely. But when it's off, you might deal with digestive issues, like bloating or indigestion, and feel a dip in your energy levels. Have you ever felt a knot in your stomach before a big presentation? That's your Solar Plexus Chakra reacting to stress.

The **Heart Chakra** plays a pivotal role in emotional health. Situated in the center of your chest, it governs your ability to love and be loved. It's the emotional core, fostering resilience and compassion. When balanced, you feel open, loving, and emotionally stable. But when blocked, you might experience emotional numbness or difficulty forming deep connections. Have you ever felt a physical ache in your chest during heartbreak? That's your Heart Chakra signaling an imbalance.

Communication is the domain of the **Throat Chakra,** located at your throat. It's all about self-expression and effective communication. When it's in balance, you speak your truth confidently and clearly. But when it's off, you might struggle to express your thoughts or even experience a sore throat. Have you ever felt a lump in your throat when you couldn't speak up? That's your Throat Chakra acting up.

Psychosomatic symptoms are another fascinating aspect of chakra imbalances. Anxiety often ties back to the Root Chakra. When you feel anxious, your foundation is shaky, making you feel ungrounded. Similarly, digestive issues can usually be traced to the Solar Plexus Chakra. Stress and emotional turmoil can disrupt your digestion, leading to physical symptoms. It's like your body waving a red flag, saying, "Hey, pay attention to your energy!"

Holistic health practices can offer incredible support for balancing your chakras. Yoga, for example, is fantastic for enhancing energy flow. Specific poses target different chakras, helping to unblock and balance them. Meditation is another powerful tool for emotional healing. By focusing your mind and calming your thoughts, you can bring harmony to your energy centers. And let's not forget about breathing exercises. Simple techniques like deep diaphragmatic breathing can reduce stress and promote overall well-being.

Imagine starting your day with a few minutes of mindful breathing and a short yoga routine targeting your main energy centers. Not only would this set a positive tone for your day, but it would also help maintain your chakra balance. Whether you're dealing with physical issues or emotional turbulence, understanding the mind-body connection through the lens of chakras can be a game-changer.

Recognizing Unbalanced Chakras: Symptoms and Signs

Recognizing the signs of unbalanced chakras is like being your energy detective. Let's start with physical symptoms, as they're often the most noticeable. Have you ever had a pounding headache that made you feel like your brain was trying to escape your skull? That might be your **Third Eye** Chakra throwing a tantrum. This chakra, located between your eyebrows, governs intuition and mental clarity. You might experience frequent headaches, blurred vision, or sinus issues when it's out of balance. Lower back pain, on the other hand, is often linked to the Root Chakra. This energy center, found at the base of your spine, is all about grounding and physical stability. When it's blocked, you might feel like your foundation is crumbling, manifesting as lower back pain, leg issues, or even problems with your feet.

Now, let's talk about emotions. Anxiety is a big red flag for an unbalanced Root Chakra. When this chakra is off-kilter, you might feel like you're constantly standing on shaky ground, leading to fear and insecurity. It's like trying to walk on a tightrope without a safety net. Emotional numbness, on the other hand, often points to issues with the Heart Chakra. This chakra, located in the center of your chest, is your emotional epicenter. You might find connecting with others or feeling genuine emotions hard when blocked. A wall has been built around your heart, keeping love and compassion out.

Behavioral symptoms can be just as telling. Overeating is a classic sign of an imbalanced Solar Plexus Chakra. This energy center in your upper abdomen governs your sense of personal power and self-esteem. When it's off, you might use food as a way to fill the void, trying to regain a sense of control and comfort. Communication issues often indicate a blocked Throat

Chakra. This chakra might need some attention if you struggle to express your thoughts or constantly feel misunderstood. It's like having a lump in your throat that won't go away, preventing you from speaking your truth.

So, how do you figure out which chakras need balancing? Self-assessment techniques can be incredibly helpful. Start with simple quizzes or checklists. These can guide you through a series of questions about physical symptoms, emotional states, and behavioral patterns, helping you pinpoint which chakras might be out of balance. For example, if you frequently experience headaches and have trouble trusting your intuition, your Third Eye Chakra might be the culprit.

Guided journaling prompts are another excellent tool for self-assessment. They encourage you to reflect on various aspects of your life and how they relate to each chakra. For instance, a prompt might ask, "When was the last time you felt truly grounded and secure?" Your response can provide insight into the state of your Root Chakra. These prompts can help you dig deeper into your emotions and behaviors, revealing patterns that might indicate chakra imbalances.

Body scanning meditation is a fantastic technique for bringing awareness to your energy centers. Find a quiet space, sit comfortably, and close your eyes. Take a few deep breaths and slowly guide your attention from the top of your head to the tips of your toes. As you focus on each area of your body, notice any sensations, discomfort, or tension. This practice can help you identify where energy might be blocked or stagnant. For example, if you feel tightness in your chest, your Heart Chakra might need love and attention.

Understanding and recognizing the symptoms of unbalanced chakras is the first step toward achieving harmony and well-being. By paying attention to physical, emotional, and behavioral signs, you can take proactive steps to restore balance and promote a healthier, more vibrant life.

Ready to see where your energy is at? Take a moment to try these simple chakra assessments and quizzes. It's a fun and easy way to check if your chakras are balanced—or if one might need extra love. Let's dive in and see where your energy stands. Who knows, your Root Chakra might just be screaming for a reboot.

Chakra Self-Assessment Checklist

Use this checklist to assess which chakras might be out of balance quickly. Answer **Yes** or **No** for each question.

1. Root Chakra (Base of the Spine)

- Do you often feel anxious, insecure, or unstable in your life?

- Do you have frequent issues with lower back pain or leg problems?

- Do you feel disconnected from your body or lack a sense of grounding?

  ☐ Yes
  ☐ No

---

2. Sacral Chakra (Below the Navel)

- Do you struggle to express your emotions or connect with others intimately?

- Are you experiencing a lack of creativity or passion in life?

- Do you have reproductive or urinary issues?

☐ Yes

☐ No

---

3. Solar Plexus Chakra (Above the Navel)

- Do you often feel powerless, lack confidence, or have trouble asserting yourself?

- Do you suffer from digestive problems or low energy?

- Do you feel stuck in taking action or pursuing your goals?

  ☐ Yes
  ☐ No

---

4. Heart Chakra (Center of the Chest)

- Do you find it hard to give or receive love openly?

- Do you struggle with forgiveness—either of yourself or others?

- Do you feel emotionally blocked or disconnected from others?

  ☐ Yes
  ☐ No

---

5. Throat Chakra (Throat Area)

- Do you have difficulty expressing your thoughts or speaking up for yourself?

- Do you often experience sore throats or issues with your voice?

- Do you need help communicating your needs and desires?

  ☐ Yes

  ☐ No

---

6. Third Eye Chakra (Forehead, Between the Eyebrows)

- Do you have trouble trusting your intuition or making decisions?

- Do you suffer from frequent headaches, eye issues, or trouble concentrating?

- Do you feel disconnected from your inner guidance or need more mental clarity?

  ☐ Yes

  ☐ No

---

7. Crown Chakra (Top of the Head)

- Do you feel disconnected from a sense of purpose or higher consciousness?

- Do you feel mentally foggy or spiritually out of touch?

- Are you experiencing difficulty connecting to something greater than yourself?

☐ Yes
☐ No

Chakra Quiz

After completing the checklist, count how often you answered "Yes" to each chakra. Here's a quick quiz to help you interpret your results:

1. If you answered **yes** to most questions about any specific chakra, that chakra may be out of balance.

2. If multiple chakras have a **Yes** response, it could indicate an overall energy imbalance or blockages.

3. **No "Yes" answers?** You may have a well-balanced energy system, but checking in regularly is essential to maintaining harmony.

How to Use This Checklist and Quiz

After identifying which chakras might be out of balance based on your "Yes" responses, you can focus on specific practices to help realign and balance those chakras. Whether it's through meditation, chakra healing exercises, or energy work, this simple self-assessment can help you better understand your energy flow and promote personal growth.

The History of Chakra Healing: From Ancient Texts to Modern Practices

Isn't it fascinating how ancient wisdom still holds so much relevance today? The concept of chakras dates back thousands of years, with its roots firmly planted in ancient Indian texts. The Vedas, some of the oldest known scriptures, provide the earliest mentions of these energy centers. Written in Sanskrit, the Vedas describe chakras as vital energy points within the body, crucial for maintaining balance and harmony. The Upanishads, part of the Vedic texts, delve deeper into the spiritual and philosophical aspects of chakras. These texts illustrate how interconnected our physical and spiritual selves are, painting a holistic picture of human well-being.

Moving forward in time, references to chakras also appear in Tantric texts. Tantra, often misunderstood in the West, encompasses a broad range of spiritual practices to attain higher states of consciousness. These texts offer more detailed descriptions of the chakras, including their locations, functions, and how they influence our lives. They also introduce techniques for balancing and activating these energy centers, laying the groundwork for modern practices.

Chakra healing has evolved significantly over the centuries. In ancient India, the development of Ayurveda and yoga played a pivotal role in this evolution. Ayurveda, the traditional system of medicine, uses herbs, diet, and lifestyle practices to balance the chakras and promote health. Yoga, with its various postures and breathing techniques, aims to keep these energy centers open and flowing. Both systems emphasize the importance of maintaining balance between body, mind, and spirit.

As the world became more interconnected, these ancient practices reached the West. Initially, they were met with skepticism, but they gained acceptance and popularity over time. The twentieth century saw a surge in interest in holistic health, leading to the integration of chakra healing into modern wellness practices. Today, you can find chakra-balancing techniques from yoga studios to self-help literature. The idea of tuning into your body's energy centers has become a mainstream approach to overall well-being.

Several notable figures have made significant contributions to our understanding of chakras. Dr. Hiroshi Motoyama, a Japanese researcher, conducted extensive studies on the relationship between chakras and physiological functions. His work provided a scientific basis for understanding how these energy centers influence our health. Motoyama's research bridged the gap between Eastern spiritual practices and Western scientific inquiry, making chakra healing more accessible globally.

Another key figure is Anodea Judith, whose books and teachings have been instrumental in popularizing chakra work in the West. With a background in psychology and health, Judith has an uncanny ability to explain complex concepts in an engaging and easy-to-understand way. Her contributions have made chakra healing more approachable for everyday folks, offering practical tools and insights that anyone can use. Judith's work emphasizes the psychological aspects of chakras, helping people understand how these energy centers affect their emotions and behaviors.

Today, chakra healing continues to adapt and evolve. Modern holistic health practices incorporate chakra work into various therapies, from Reiki to sound healing. Wellness literature often includes sections on chakras, offering readers simple exercises and meditations to balance their energy. Integrating ancient wisdom with contemporary practices creates a rich tapestry of healing modalities, providing multiple pathways to well-being.

Reflecting on the history of chakra healing, it's clear that this ancient wisdom has stood the test of time for good reason. Its principles are universal, transcending cultural and temporal boundaries. Whether you're practicing yoga, reading a self-help book, or visiting a holistic healer, the essence of chakra work remains the same: to promote balance, harmony, and a deeper connection with yourself. As you continue exploring this fascinating subject, remember that you're tapping into a tradition that has enriched lives for millennia. And that, my friend, is pretty amazing.

Chapter 2:
Techniques for Balancing Chakras

When I first started meditating, I remember sitting cross-legged on my living room floor, determined to become a Zen master in one day. Spoiler alert: i-It didn't happen. Instead, my mind wandered to my grocery list, to-do list, and why my dogs were staring at me with such intensity. It wasn't until I discovered chakra meditation that things began to click. Suddenly, meditation had a purpose beyond just "being calm." It became a way to balance my energy and feel more centered in my chaotic life. Let's dive into how you can use meditation specifically for chakra healing.

Meditation for Chakra Healing: Techniques and Benefits

Chakra meditation is a targeted practice designed to balance and align your energy centers or chakras. Unlike general meditation, which often focuses on mindfulness or relaxation, chakra meditation zeroes in on each of the seven chakras, aiming to clear blockages and enhance energy flow. The purpose is to bring harmony to your physical, emotional, and spiritual self. Think of it as tuning your body like a musical instrument, ensuring each string plays a harmonious note.

How do you meditate to balance your chakras? Let's break it down.

- Start with the **Root Chakra**, located at the base of your spine. Find a comfortable seated position, close your eyes, and take a few deep breaths. Focus on the base of your spine and visualize a red, spinning wheel. Imagine roots growing from your spine into the ground, anchoring you. Feel the stability and grounding this provides. Spend a few minutes here, breathing deeply and visualizing the color red.

- Next, move to the **Heart Chakra**, located in the center of your chest. Visualize a green, glowing light expanding from your heart. Feel the warmth and love radiating outward. Think about someone you love or a cherished memory. Let this feeling of compassion and connection fill your entire being. This practice opens your Heart Chakra and fosters emotional healing and balance.

- Finally, focus on the **Crown Chakra** at the top of your head. Visualize a violet or white light pouring into the top of your head, connecting you to the universe. Feel a sense of peace and spiritual connection. This meditation enhances your spiritual awareness, making you feel more connected to something greater than yourself.

The benefits of chakra meditation are numerous. For one, it significantly improves emotional balance. Focusing on each chakra addresses specific emotional issues tied to that energy center. For instance, balancing the Heart Chakra can help you process grief and foster forgiveness. Physically, chakra meditation can lead to enhanced health. When your energy flows freely, it promotes better circulation, reduces stress, and alleviates chronic pain. Spiritually, this practice increases your awareness and connection to higher consciousness, providing a deeper sense of purpose and fulfillment.

Of course, meditation isn't without its challenges. Many people struggle with focusing, especially in the beginning. If you find your mind wandering, consider using guided meditations. Plenty of apps and online resources with guided sessions can help keep you on track. Another common issue is discomfort during meditation. If sitting cross-legged feels like a medieval torture method, try adjusting your posture. Use cushions to support your back or sit in a chair. The goal is to be comfortable enough to focus, not to endure unnecessary pain.

Here are a few guided meditation app suggestions that are gentle on the budget while helping you find peace and balance:

1. Insight Timer

- **Cost**: Free with optional in-app purchases.

- **Why it's excellent**: Insight Timer is known for its vast library of over 100,000 free guided meditations. It also offers customizable meditation timers, music, and talks from mindfulness teachers worldwide. You can access most features without a subscription.

- **It is best for**: People looking for variety and extensive free content.

2. Smiling Mind

- **Cost**: Completely free.

- **Why it's excellent**: Smiling Mind is a nonprofit app designed to make mindfulness and meditation accessible to everyone. It offers programs for children, teenagers, and adults, making it ideal for families. There are no hidden fees or subscription models.

- **It is best for:** Beginners, kids, and families looking for structured mindfulness programs.

3. MyLife (Formerly Stop, Breathe & Think)

- **Cost**: Free with optional premium upgrades.

- **Why it's excellent**: MyLife offers a personalized meditation experience based on your feelings. Many of its meditation practices and mindfulness exercises are free, including breathing exercises and stress relief tools. The app recommends meditations based on your emotional check-in.

- **It is best for:** Those looking for personalized mindfulness recommendations based on mood.

Of course, there are many other options, but some might ask for a tiny monthly or annual love (aka a fee). It all comes down to what you're looking for and how deep you want to dive into your practice. My advice? Start with the free ones—you'll be surprised how much you love them! Then, if you're ready to go all-in, you can explore the paid versions later. No rush; your chakras will still be there!

Interactive Element: Guided Chakra Meditation Script

Find a quiet space where you won't be disturbed. Sit comfortably, close your eyes, and take a few deep breaths in … and out. Let's begin.

Root Chakra

*Focus on the base of your spine. Visualize a red, spinning wheel of energy. As you breathe deeply, say to yourself, **"I am grounded. I am safe."** Imagine the warmth and heaviness of your body being pulled gently toward the earth. Feel stability and support beneath you with each breath, like the earth is holding you. You might even press your feet firmly on the ground to strengthen that connection. Feel the security this brings.*

Heart Chakra

*Now, move your attention to the center of your chest. Visualize a glowing green light. Place your hand on your chest, and as you breathe deeply, say, **"I am loved. I am open to giving and receiving love."** Imagine this light expanding, filling your entire chest with warmth. Think of someone or something that brings you joy. Feel your chest expand with love, gratitude,* *and kindness, sending that love outward, radiating through your body and beyond.*

Crown Chakra

Shift your focus to the top of your head, the Crown Chakra. Visualize a soft violet or white light entering through the crown of your head. As you breathe, say to yourself, **"I am connected to the universe. I trust in the flow of life."** *Feel a gentle tingling sensation at the top of your head, like a soft breeze or a gentle touch. Let this light flow through your entire being, filling you with peace and clarity, connecting you to something greater than yourself.*

Take a few more deep breaths here, feeling your energy balanced and your body grounded. When you're ready, slowly open your eyes and return to the present moment.

Incorporating affirmations, hand placement, and breath awareness can help guide the mind and body into a deeper state of connection with each chakra.

Meditation is a journey, not a destination. Don't be discouraged if it takes time to feel the benefits. The key is consistency. Practice regularly, even if it's just for a few minutes each day. Over time, you'll notice a difference in how you feel emotionally and physically. And remember, it's perfectly okay to have days where meditation feels challenging. The important thing is to keep going.

The Power of Visualization: Guided Chakra Imagery

You know that feeling when you close your eyes and imagine yourself on a beach, the sound of waves lapping at the shore, and, suddenly, you feel a sense of calm wash over you? That's the power of visualization. Visualization uses mental imagery to balance and align your energy centers in chakra healing. It's like a mental workout for your chakras, helping to restore harmony and improve your overall well-being. Visualization involves picturing specific images, colors, and sensations associated with each chakra, directing your focus to those areas, and allowing the energy to flow freely.

One significant benefit of guided imagery is that it provides a structured way to focus your mind, making it easier to engage with each chakra. Guided visualization offers a step-by-step approach, often narrated, that helps you concentrate on each energy center, making the process accessible even for beginners. Using guided imagery, you can tap into the subconscious mind, facilitating emotional release and healing. This technique can enhance your focus and clarity, providing a mental map to navigate your inner landscape.

Let's start with the Root Chakra, located at the base of your spine. Imagine standing in a lush forest, feeling the solid earth beneath your feet. Visualize roots growing from your body into the ground, anchoring you firmly. These roots provide stability and nourishment, connecting you deeply to the earth. Feel the strength and groundedness this brings, allowing any insecurity or fear to dissipate. This exercise helps you connect with your foundation, promoting safety and stability.

Next, focus on the Solar Plexus Chakra in your upper abdomen. Picture a bright, glowing sun at your solar plexus, radiating warmth and light. This sun represents your power and confidence. As you breathe in, imagine the sun growing brighter, filling you with a sense of empowerment and determination. Visualize this light spreading through your body, igniting your inner strength and willpower. This visualization enhances your self-esteem and helps you tackle challenges with confidence.

For the Third Eye Chakra, located between your eyebrows, envision a radiant indigo light on your forehead. This light represents your intuition and inner wisdom. Imagine it pulsing gently, growing brighter with each breath. Feel this light expanding, clearing any fog or confusion from your mind. As the light intensifies, it sharpens your perception and insight, allowing you to see things clearly and intuitively. This exercise helps you tap into your inner guidance, promoting mental clarity and spiritual awareness.

Using visualization techniques offers several benefits. It enhances your focus and clarity by providing a clear mental image to concentrate on, making it easier to engage with each chakra. Visualization also facilitates emotional release and healing, allowing you to bring subconscious issues to the surface and address them. Regularly practicing these techniques can improve your emotional balance and overall well-being.

Incorporate sensory details to make your visualization practice more effective. Engage your senses by imagining the visual aspects and the sounds, smells, and sensations associated with each chakra. For example, imagine the earthy scent of the forest and the sound of leaves rustling when visualizing the Root Chakra. This multisensory approach makes the visualization more vivid and immersive, enhancing its impact.

Consistency is critical to effective visualization. Make it a regular part of your routine, even if it's just for a few minutes each day. The more you practice, the more natural it will feel and the more benefits you'll experience. Start with short sessions and gradually extend them as you become more comfortable with the technique. Over time, visualization becomes a powerful tool for balancing your chakras and improving your overall well-being.

One practical tip is to create a dedicated space for your visualization practice. Find a quiet, comfortable spot where you won't be disturbed. Use props like cushions or blankets to make yourself comfortable. You can also set the mood with soft lighting or calming music. This creates a conducive environment for your practice, making it easier to focus and relax.

As mentioned, these apps are *fantastic,* and as a bonus, they're all free! **Insight Timer** is a treasure trove of free guided visualizations that'll have you tapping into your inner calm in no time. **Smiling Mind** is perfect for the whole family, offering mindfulness programs that make meditation fun and easy. And **MyLife** is your personalized meditation sidekick, giving you guided imagery based on your mood (because, let's face it, sometimes you're not sure which chakra needs a time-out). Best part? Your wallet stays happy, too!

Yoga Poses for Each Chakra: Enhancing Energy Flow

When I first started exploring yoga, I was overwhelmed by all the different poses and their supposed benefits. It wasn't until I learned about chakra-specific yoga that things began to make sense. Yoga and chakras are like peanut butter and jelly—they just go together. Yoga poses, or asanas, influence energy flow through your body, helping to balance and align your chakras. Each pose targets specific energy centers, promoting physical, emotional, and spiritual well-being. The importance of breath and alignment in yoga can't be overstated. Proper breathing (pranayama) and alignment ensure that energy flows freely, enhancing the effectiveness of each pose.

Let's break it down:

We're starting with the Root Chakra. This energy center, located at the base of your spine, benefits immensely from grounding poses. Mountain Pose (Tadasana) is a great starting point. Stand with your feet hip-width apart, arms at your sides, and focus on feeling the ground beneath you. Imagine roots growing from your feet into the earth, grounding you. Warrior Pose (Virabhadrasana) is another excellent pose for this chakra. Stand with your feet wide apart, turn your right foot out, and bend your right knee. Extend your arms parallel to the ground and gaze over your right hand. Feel the strength and stability this pose provides, grounding you firmly.

Next, we move to the Sacral Chakra, located in the lower abdomen. This chakra thrives on poses that open the hips and encourage fluidity. Bound Angle Pose (Baddha Konasana) is perfect for this. Sit on the ground, bring the soles of your feet together, and let your knees fall open. Hold your feet with your hands and gently press your knees toward the floor. Seated Forward Bend (Paschimottanasana) is another beneficial pose. Sit with your legs extended in front of you, inhale and lengthen your spine, exhale, and fold forward, reaching for your toes. These poses help release stored emotions and enhance creativity.

Heart-opening poses are essential for the Heart Chakra, located in the center of your chest. Camel Pose (Ustrasana) is a powerful heart opener. Kneel on the floor with your knees hip-width apart. Place your hands on your lower back for support, inhale, and lift your chest as you arch your back. If comfortable, reach your hands back to touch your heels. Bridge Pose (Setu Bandhasana) is another excellent choice. Lie on your back with your knees bent and feet hip-width apart. Press into your feet to lift your hips toward the ceiling, clasping your hands under your back. These poses open your heart center, promoting love and compassion.

Incorporating yoga into your chakra healing routine offers numerous benefits. Physically, it improves flexibility and strength, making your body more resilient. Mentally, it enhances clarity and focus, helping you navigate life's challenges with a calm mind. Emotionally, it brings stability, allowing you to process and release stored emotions. Yoga helps maintain a balanced energy flow by targeting specific chakras, promoting overall well-being.

Creating a personalized chakra yoga routine can be incredibly rewarding. Start by setting an intention for your practice. This could be as simple as **"I want to feel more grounded"** or **"I aim to open my heart."** Begin your session with grounding poses like Mountain Pose and Warrior Pose to stabilize your Root Chakra. Move to hip openers for the Sacral Chakra, such as Bound Angle Pose and Seated Forward Bend. Incorporate heart openers like Camel Pose and Bridge Pose for the Heart Chakra.

Combine these poses into full practice, flowing from one to the next with mindful breath and alignment. Ensure you spend equal time on each chakra, maintaining balance throughout your session. You can also add poses for the other chakras, like Boat Pose for the Solar Plexus Chakra or Fish Pose for the Throat Chakra. The key is to listen to your body and adjust as needed.

Incorporating these yoga poses into your daily routine can help you maintain a balanced and harmonious energy flow, enhancing your overall well-being. Remember, consistency is critical. Regular practice, even if it's just for a few minutes each day, can make a significant difference in how you feel.

Breathing Exercises: Harnessing Prana for Chakra Balance

Breathing exercises, or pranayama, are like the secret sauce of chakra healing. Pranayama comes from the Sanskrit words "prana" (life force or vital energy) and "ayama" (control). So, pranayama means controlling your life force through breath. It's a powerful tool for balancing chakras because it directly influences energy flow within your body. Different pranayama techniques can target specific chakras, helping to clear blockages and enhance energy flow. Prana, this unseen life force, keeps us alive and vibrant. When prana flows freely, you feel energized and balanced. When it's blocked, you might feel sluggish or emotionally drained.

Deep diaphragmatic breathing is one of the simplest yet most effective pranayama techniques for balancing the *Root Chakra*. Sit comfortably with your spine straight. Place one hand on your chest and the other on your abdomen. Inhale deeply through your nose, filling your belly with air (your hand on the abdomen should rise while the hand on the chest stays still). Exhale slowly through your mouth. This breathing helps ground you, bringing a sense of stability and security. It's beneficial when you're anxious or ungrounded, like when life throws you a curveball.

For the *Throat Chakra*, try Ujjayi breath, also known as the Victorious breath. This technique involves slightly constricting the back of your throat while you breathe, creating a soft, ocean-like sound. Sit comfortably and inhale deeply through your nose, then exhale while keeping the throat slightly constricted. This breath helps clear the Throat Chakra, improving your ability to communicate and express yourself. It's perfect when you need to find your voice during a tough conversation or a public speaking event.

The *Crown Chakra* benefits immensely from alternate nostril breathing or Nadi Shodhana. This technique balances the energy flow between your brain's left and right hemispheres, promoting a sense of calm and spiritual connection. Sit comfortably and use your right thumb to close your right nostril. Inhale deeply through your left nostril, then close the left nostril with your right ring finger and exhale through the right nostril. Inhale through the right nostril, close it, and exhale through the left nostril. This completes one cycle. Repeat for several cycles. This practice enhances concentration and focus, making connecting with your higher self easier.

Pranayama offers numerous physical and emotional benefits. Physically, these breathing exercises improve oxygenation, promoting better circulation and overall health. They also help reduce stress and anxiety by activating the parasympathetic nervous system, which calms the mind and body. Emotionally, pranayama enhances your ability to focus and concentrate, making it easier to navigate life's challenges with a clear mind. When you're stressed or anxious, your breath becomes shallow and rapid. Pranayama helps reverse this, encouraging deep, slow breaths that bring a sense of calm and clarity.

Incorporating pranayama into your daily routine doesn't have to be complicated. Start with a few minutes each day and gradually increase the duration as you become more comfortable. Consistency is key. Regular practice ensures that the benefits accumulate over time, helping you maintain balanced energy and emotional stability. Find a quiet space where you won't be disturbed and sit comfortably. Proper posture is crucial for effective pranayama. Keep your spine straight and your shoulders relaxed. This allows for the free flow of energy and makes the breathing exercises more effective.

Creating a conducive environment can also enhance your practice. Use cushions or blankets to support your posture and make yourself comfortable. Set the mood with soft lighting or calming music. This creates a peaceful atmosphere, making it easier to focus on your breath and connect with your energy centers. Remember, pranayama is a practice, not a perfection. It's okay if your mind wanders or you find it challenging. The important thing is to keep practicing. Over time, pranayama becomes a powerful tool for maintaining balanced chakras and promoting overall well-being.

Sound Therapy: Using Mantras and Frequencies

Picture this: You're lying on a mat, eyes closed, and a soft, resonant hum fills the room. The sound vibrates through your body, and you can almost feel your stress melting away. That's sound therapy in action. Using sound for healing is not a new concept. It has roots in ancient cultures, from Tibetan singing bowls to the chants of Gregorian monks. Sound therapy involves using specific frequencies to balance your body's energy centers or chakras. This can be done through various methods, including mantras, singing bowls, and tuning forks.

Mantras are powerful tools in sound therapy. **Each chakra has a specific mantra**, a sacred sound that helps balance that energy center.

- The mantra for the Root Chakra is **"LAM."** Sit comfortably, close your eyes, and take a deep breath. As you exhale, chant **"LAM"** slowly and deeply. Feel the vibration in your lower body, grounding you and providing a sense of stability.

- The mantra for the Heart Chakra is **"YAM."** Chanting **"YAM"** focuses on the center of your chest, opening your heart to love and compassion.

- The mantra to use for the Third Eye Chakra is "OM." Chanting **"OM"** resonates through your forehead, enhancing your intuition and inner wisdom.

Sound therapy offers numerous benefits. Vibrational healing is at the core of this practice. Sound frequencies influence the energy centers in your body, helping to clear blockages and restore balance. When you chant a mantra or listen to a singing bowl, the sound waves travel through your body, promoting relaxation and emotional release. It's like giving your chakras a gentle massage, loosening tension, and promoting a free energy flow. Sound therapy can also reduce stress and anxiety, helping you feel more centered and at peace.

Incorporating sound therapy into your chakra healing practices can be incredibly rewarding. Start by using recorded mantras and frequencies.

Plenty of resources online, from YouTube videos to specialized apps, offer guided sound therapy sessions. You can also create a sound therapy routine. Dedicate a few minutes each day to chanting mantras or listening to healing sounds. Find a quiet space where you won't be disturbed, sit comfortably, and focus on the sound. Let the vibrations wash over you, bringing balance and harmony to your energy centers.

Here's a short list of options for mantra and sound therapy to help you begin your journey and discover the perfect sound and vibration that resonates with you.

1. YouTube

- **Why it's excellent:** Numerous free videos offer guided chakra meditations, mantras, and sound healing practices for each chakra.

- **How to find it:** Search for specific chakra mantras (e.g., "Root Chakra mantra meditation") or guided sound therapy.

2. Spotify/Apple Music

- **Why it's great:** Many playlists and albums offer chakra sound healing, including mantras and binaural beats for chakra alignment.

- **How to find it:** Search for "chakra sound healing" or "chakra mantras."

3. Insight Timer (Free Meditation App)

- **Why it's great:** This app has many free meditations, including specific chakra mantras and sound healing.

- **How to find it:** Browse the "Chakra Healing" category or search for chakra mantra meditations.

4. Calm and Headspace (Subscription Apps)

- **Why it's excellent:** Calm and Headspace provide guided meditations and soundscapes that include chakra healing mantras, especially within their sleep or focus sections.

- **How to find it:** Use the search feature in the app for "chakra sound therapy" or "mantras."

5. Chopra.com

- **Why it's excellent:** Deepak Chopra's website offers many resources on meditation, including articles, guided meditations, and mantras for chakra balancing.

- **How to find it:** Visit Chopra.com and explore the meditation section for chakra-specific content.

6. SoundCloud

- **Why it's excellent**: SoundCloud hosts a variety of sound healing and mantra creators that provide free chakra therapy audios.

- **How to find it:** Search for "chakra sound healing" or specific chakra mantras on SoundCloud.

Another effective method is using singing bowls. Tibetan singing bowls, in particular, are renowned for their healing properties. Each bowl produces a specific frequency that resonates with a different chakra. Hold a singing bowl in your hand and gently strike the rim with a mallet. Then, run the mallet around the rim in a circular motion, creating a continuous sound. Focus on the vibration and how it feels in your body. This practice can help clear blockages and enhance the flow of energy.

Scan the QR code to hear the beautiful sounds of a singing bowl, giving you insight into its soothing vibrations and how it can enhance your meditation practice. But heads up—before you get to the relaxing tones, you'll probably

have to sit through an ad or two (because what's a little Zen without a commercial break, right?). Just be patient, and the peaceful vibes will be worth the wait!

Tuning forks are also valuable tools in sound therapy. These instruments produce precise frequencies that can target specific chakras. To use a tuning fork, strike it against a hard surface to make it vibrate, then hold it near the chakra you want to balance. The sound waves will penetrate your body, promoting healing and alignment. Tuning forks are particularly effective for people who prefer a more structured approach to sound therapy.

Interactive Element: Creating Your Sound Therapy Kit

Consider assembling a sound therapy kit to enhance your practice. Include items like a set of tuning forks, a Tibetan singing bowl, and a playlist of chakra mantras. Having these tools on hand makes it easier to incorporate sound therapy into your daily routine. You can also add a comfortable mat or cushion for sitting, ensuring you're relaxed and comfortable during your sessions.

Remember, the key to effective sound therapy is consistency. Make it a regular part of your routine, even if it's just for a few minutes each day. Over time, you'll notice the benefits, from reduced stress to improved emotional balance. Sound therapy is a powerful tool for chakra healing, offering a simple yet effective way to promote well-being.

Aromatherapy: Essential Oils and Their Chakra Correspondences

Let's talk about one of my favorite topics—aromatherapy. Imagine entering a room filled with lavender's soothing scent or peppermint's refreshing aroma. Instantly, you feel a shift in your mood and energy. That's the magic of aromatherapy. At its core, aromatherapy uses essential oils extracted from plants to promote physical, emotional, and spiritual well-being. These oils are the essence of the plant, capturing its unique properties. When it comes to chakra healing, essential oils can be incredibly effective. They influence our energy centers by working directly on the limbic system—the part of the brain that controls emotions and memories—thereby affecting our overall energy balance.

Each essential oil has specific properties that align with different chakras; for the Root Chakra, which is all about stability and grounding, oils like Patchouli and Cedarwood are fantastic. Patchouli has a rich, earthy aroma that can make you feel more anchored, while Cedarwood offers a warm, woody scent that promotes a sense of security. Moving up to the Sacral Chakra, which governs creativity and emotions, Orange and Ylang Ylang are your go-to oils. Orange oil's vibrant, citrusy fragrance invigorates creativity, while Ylang Ylang's sweet, floral scent can help release emotional tension and promote joy.

When we reach the *Throat Chakra*, essential oils like Peppermint and Eucalyptus are perfect. Peppermint's cool, refreshing scent can clear mental fog and improve communication, while Eucalyptus offers a sharp, refreshing aroma that opens up the airways, making it easier to express yourself. Each chakra has specific oils that can help balance and align its energy, making aromatherapy a versatile tool in your chakra healing toolkit.

The benefits of using essential oils for chakra balancing are numerous.

- First and foremost, they enhance relaxation and relieve stress. Imagine coming home after a long day, diffusing some lavender oil, and instantly feeling the tension melt away. Essential oils can also improve emotional well-being. Scents like Rose or Jasmine can uplift your mood and make you feel more positive. The olfactory system—your sense of smell—is directly connected to the limbic system in your brain, which is why scents can have such a powerful impact on your emotions.

- Using essential oils in your daily life is easier than you might think. One practical way is to diffuse the oils in your living spaces. A diffuser disperses the essential oil into the air, allowing you to breathe it in and benefit from its properties throughout the day. For instance, you can diffuse lavender in your bedroom to promote restful sleep or peppermint in your workspace to enhance focus and clarity. Another practical application is the topical use of essential oils. Always dilute them with a carrier oil like coconut or jojoba oil to avoid skin irritation. You can apply these blends to specific chakra points. For example, rub a diluted mixture of Patchouli and Cedarwood on your lower back to ground your Root Chakra.

- Creating personalized blends tailored to your needs can be a fun and rewarding experience. Let's say you want to boost your creativity while maintaining emotional balance. Mix Orange, Ylang Ylang, and carrier oil in a small roller bottle. Apply this blend to your lower abdomen and wrists whenever you need a creative boost or emotional lift. This way, you're enjoying the delightful scents and actively working to balance your chakras.

- Aromatherapy can be a game-changer in your chakra healing practice, providing an easy and enjoyable way to influence your energy centers. The key is consistently finding and incorporating the scents that resonate with you into your daily routine. Whether you're diffusing oils, applying them topically, or creating personalized blends, you'll find that these aromatic allies can significantly enhance your overall well-being.

- Understanding the role of aromatherapy and the specific essential oils that correspond to each chakra can help you create a more balanced and harmonious energy flow. This helps relieve stress, improve emotional well-being, and enhance your spiritual connection and overall quality of life. So, take a moment to explore the world of essential oils and see how they can support your journey toward chakra balance and holistic wellness.

Chapter 3:
Tools and Elements for Chakra Healing

Have you ever found yourself wandering through a crystal shop, mesmerized by the kaleidoscope of colors and shapes but utterly clueless about what to do with them? I've been there, too. My first experience was like stepping into Aladdin's cave of shimmering magic with no genie to guide me. But I was hooked once I discovered how these beautiful stones could balance my chakras. Let's dive into the fascinating world of crystals and gemstones and explore how they can enhance your chakra healing journey.

Crystals and Gemstones: Selecting and Using for Each Chakra

Crystals have been used for healing and protection for thousands of years. Over 6,000 years ago, the ancient Sumerians incorporated crystals into their magical formulas. The Egyptians, too, were fans, using them for health and protection and even placing them in tombs to guide the dead. Fast forward to the modern era, and crystals are often seen as mystical tools that can interact with our energy fields. While scientific evidence supporting their efficacy is lacking, many people swear by their positive effects, attributing changes in their well-being to these shimmering stones.

So, how do these crystals work? Think of your body as a complex energy system, with chakras as energy hubs. Crystals are believed to resonate with these energy centers, helping to clear blockages and restore balance. Each crystal has its own unique vibrational frequency, which can interact with your body's energy field, promoting healing and harmony.

When selecting crystals for each chakra, start with the basics.

- For the ***Root Chakra***, located at the base of your spine, think of grounding stones like Red Jasper and Hematite. Red Jasper provides stability and strength with its deep, earthy hues, while Hematite, with its metallic sheen, is fantastic for grounding and protection.

- Moving up to the ***Sacral Chakra,*** nestled in your lower abdomen, opt for stones like Carnelian and Orange Calcite. Carnelian's vibrant orange energizes creativity and passion, while Orange Calcite's gentle energy promotes emotional balance.

- For the ***Crown Chakra***, perched at the top of your head, Amethyst and Clear Quartz are your best friends. Amethyst, with its regal purple tones, enhances spiritual awareness and tranquility. Clear Quartz, often regarded as the master healer, amplifies energy and thought, promoting clarity and connection to higher consciousness.

There are various ways to use crystals for chakra healing. One effective method is placing crystals directly on specific chakras during meditation. Lie comfortably, place the crystal on the chakra you wish to balance, and focus on your breath. Visualize the crystal's energy merging with your own, clearing blockages and restoring harmony. Wearing crystal jewelry is another practical approach. A necklace with a pendant that rests over your heart can help balance the Heart Chakra, while a bracelet with beads corresponding to different chakras can provide overall energy alignment.

Another powerful technique is creating crystal grids. Arrange your chosen crystals in a geometric pattern on a sacred space, like an altar or a dedicated corner of your room. Each crystal in the grid amplifies the energy of the others, creating a potent field of healing energy. This method is particularly effective for setting intentions and manifesting goals.

Crystals need regular cleansing and charging to maintain their efficacy. Think of it as a spa day for your stones. Cleansing removes any negative energy they may have absorbed while charging and restores their vibrational frequency. There are several methods for cleansing crystals. Water is a popular choice—simply rinse your crystals under running water for a few minutes. Sunlight and moonlight are also effective. Place your crystals in direct sunlight or moonlight for a few hours. Earth burial is another method; bury your crystals in the earth for twenty-four hours to cleanse and recharge them. Sound cleansing can also be effective using a singing bowl or tuning fork.

Here's a quick guide to help you discover which crystals are recommended for balancing and healing each chakra:

1. Root Chakra (Muladhara)

- **Crystals**: Red Jasper, Hematite, Smoky Quartz

- **Insight**: The Root Chakra, located at the base of the spine, is all about grounding, stability, and survival. **Red Jasper** provides strength, courage, and endurance, making it great for staying grounded during stressful times. **Hematite**, with its metallic sheen, offers powerful grounding energy and protection, helping to anchor you firmly to the earth. **Smoky Quartz** clears negativity and grounds your energy to the earth, perfect for reconnecting to your base.

2. Sacral Chakra (Svadhisthana)

- **Crystals**: Carnelian, Orange Calcite, Tiger's Eye

- **Insight**: The Sacral Chakra governs creativity, passion, and emotional balance. **With** its vibrant orange hue, Carnelian stimulates creativity, passion, and courage, helping restore emotional balance. **Orange Calcite** enhances emotional healing and clears blockages, promoting joy and creative flow. **Tiger's Eye** is another powerful stone that balances emotional energies and strengthens willpower, making it perfect for this chakra.

3. Solar Plexus Chakra (Manipura)

- **Crystals**: Citrine, Yellow Jasper, Pyrite

- **Insight**: The Solar Plexus Chakra, located above the navel, is about personal power, confidence, and self-worth. **Citrine** is the go-to stone for boosting confidence and manifesting success, empowering the Solar Plexus to radiate positivity. **Yellow Jasper** promotes self-assurance and stability, reinforcing inner strength. **Pyrite** is known as "fool's gold," but its energy is anything but—it strengthens determination and helps attract abundance.

4. Heart Chakra (Anahata)

- **Crystals**: Rose Quartz, Green Aventurine, Rhodonite

- **Insight**: The Heart Chakra, located at the center of your chest, is about love, compassion, and emotional healing. **Rose Quartz** is the ultimate stone of unconditional love, helping heal emotional wounds and opening your heart to giving and receiving love. **Green Aventurine** promotes emotional calm and encourages healing through compassion and balance. **Rhodonite** is fantastic for healing heartbreak and nurturing self-love.

5. Throat Chakra (Vishuddha)

- **Crystals**: Blue Lace Agate, Lapis Lazuli, Aquamarine

- **Insight**: The Throat Chakra governs communication, self-expression, and truth. **Blue Lace Agate** is a gentle stone that calms and encourages clear communication, making it easier to speak your truth confidently. **Lapis Lazuli** enhances intellectual ability and aids in clear, articulate self-expression while boosting wisdom and insight. **Aquamarine** helps you express your truth while staying calm and composed, perfect for emotional conversations.

6. Third Eye Chakra (Ajna)

- **Crystals**: Amethyst, Labradorite, Sodalite

- **Insight**: The Third Eye Chakra is located between the eyebrows and is linked to intuition, wisdom, and inner vision. **Amethyst** enhances spiritual awareness and intuition, helping you tap into higher consciousness and gain deeper insights. **Labradorite** is known for awakening psychic abilities and enhancing clarity of thought, making it ideal for exploring your intuitive gifts. **Sodalite** improves mental clarity and trust in your inner guidance, encouraging balanced insights.

7. Crown Chakra (Sahasrara)

- **Crystals**: Clear Quartz, Selenite, Amethyst

- **Insight**: The Crown Chakra, located at the top of the head, is all about spiritual connection, enlightenment, and higher consciousness. **Clear Quartz** is known as the "Master Healer" and can cleanse, amplify, and balance energy, making it a perfect stone for opening the Crown Chakra and connecting it to divine energy. **Selenite** brings a high vibrational connection to spiritual realms and purifies your energy, while **Amethyst** also assists in spiritual awakening and inner peace.

Crystals aren't just pretty stones to keep on your shelf—they have some seriously incredible stories and powers that might surprise you! From protecting ancient warriors in battle to being used in sacred rituals for thousands of years, crystals have done it all. And when it comes to healing your chakras, they offer more than meets the eye.

If you want to build a crystal collection for chakra healing, asking the right questions will help you select stones that align with your energy and healing goals. Here are some essential questions to guide you:

1. What areas of my life or energy feel unbalanced?

- Consider which chakras might be blocked or out of alignment. For example, if you're feeling anxious or ungrounded, you may need crystals for the Root Chakra, like Red Jasper or Hematite.

2. What emotions or challenges am I currently dealing with?

- Emotional challenges often correspond to specific chakras. If you're struggling with creativity or emotional expression, stones for the Sacral Chakra, like Carnelian or Orange Calcite, may be helpful.

3. What kind of healing or intention do I want to focus on?

- Determine what you want to achieve with your crystals: emotional balance, spiritual growth, physical healing, or protection. This will help guide your selection.

4. Which chakra do I feel most drawn to working with?

- Intuition can play a significant role in choosing crystals. Trust your gut when selecting stones—sometimes, you'll feel an inexplicable pull toward a crystal that resonates with a specific chakra.

5. What properties or energies do these crystals offer?

- Research the healing properties of crystals to ensure they align with your needs. For instance, Amethyst is excellent for Crown

Chakra healing and enhancing spiritual awareness, while Rose Quartz is ideal for Heart Chakra work and fostering self-love.

6. Do I want to use crystals during meditation, wear them as jewelry, or create a crystal grid?

- Consider how you'll incorporate these crystals into your chakra healing practice. Some stones are perfect for placing on chakras during meditation, while others work well as jewelry for continuous energy alignment.

7. How do I cleanse and charge these crystals?

- Ask yourself if you're comfortable with each crystal's cleansing and charging methods, whether through the moonlight, sunlight, or water, and how often you'll need to refresh your energy.

8. Am I open to working with crystals that heal multiple chakras?

- Some stones, like Clear Quartz, are versatile and can balance multiple chakras simultaneously. If you're new to crystal healing, consider starting with crystals covering a broader chakra work range.

9. How do I feel when I hold or wear this crystal?

- Pay attention to how the crystal makes you feel when you first hold or wear it. The right crystal for chakra healing will resonate with your energy and create a sense of peace, warmth, or balance.

10. Do I need specific crystals for each chakra, or do I want to build a general healing set?

- Decide if you want to build a collection that targets specific chakras, like a stone for each energy center, or if you'd prefer a set of crystals that promote overall balance and well-being.

Healing Herbs and Teas: Nature's Support for Energy Centers

Have you ever thought about how the simple act of sipping herbal tea could realign your energy and balance your chakras? It might sound like a scene out of a fairy tale, but the connection between herbs and chakra health is ancient and profound. Herbs have been used for centuries to influence both physical and energetic health. They can offer a gentle, natural way to support your body's energy centers, promoting balance and harmony.

Herbs work their magic by interacting with our physical and energetic systems. Depending on your body's needs, they contain compounds that can invigorate, calm, or cleanse. When you drink herbal tea, you're not just soothing your throat or calming your nerves but also nourishing your energy centers. These herbs can enhance energy flow through your chakras, helping to clear blockages and restore balance. Herbal teas, in particular, are an excellent way to incorporate these benefits into your daily routine, providing both hydration and healing.

Let's explore some herbs that correspond to specific chakras:

1. Root Chakra (Muladhara)

- **Herbs**: Dandelion Root, Ashwagandha, Clove, and Hibiscus

- **Insight**: The Root Chakra, located at the base of the spine, is all about grounding, stability, and survival. Herbs with deep, earthy qualities can help you feel more connected to the earth and secure in your body. **Dandelion root tea**, for instance, can help detoxify and ground you, while **Ashwagandha** is known for reducing stress and promoting physical and energetic stability.

2. Sacral Chakra (Svadhisthana)

- **Herbs**: Cinnamon, Hibiscus, Calendula, and Damiana

- **Insight**: The Sacral Chakra, located in the lower abdomen, governs creativity, pleasure, and emotional balance. Herbs with warming and stimulating qualities can enhance creativity and passion. **Cinnamon** and **Damiana tea** stimulate this chakra by enhancing pleasure, sensuality, and emotional balance. **Hibiscus** adds a sweet, uplifting flavor that stirs passion and joy.

3. Solar Plexus Chakra (Manipura)

- **Herbs**: Ginger, Chamomile, Turmeric, and Lemongrass

- **Insight**: The Solar Plexus Chakra, located just above the navel, is all about confidence, personal power, and digestion. Herbs that stimulate digestion and build inner strength are ideal. **Ginger tea** is excellent for firing this chakra, promoting physical digestion and empowerment. **Chamomile** calms the digestive system, bringing warmth and relaxation and encouraging confidence and clarity.

4. Heart Chakra (Anahata)

- **Herbs**: Rose, Hawthorn, Lavender, and Jasmine

- **Insight**: The Heart Chakra, located in the center of your chest, governs love, compassion, and emotional healing. Delicate floral herbs help open the heart and promote emotional balance. **Rose tea** is particularly effective in healing emotional wounds and encouraging love for yourself and others. **Hawthorn** is often used for heart health and can help open the Heart Chakra for deeper connections.

5. Throat Chakra (Vishuddha)

- **Herbs**: Peppermint, Eucalyptus, Thyme, and Sage

- **Insight**: The Throat Chakra, located in the throat area, is about communication, self-expression, and truth. Herbs that soothe the throat and support clear breathing are ideal for this chakra. **Peppermint tea** helps clear any blockages in communication and can soothe a sore throat, promoting clearer speech. **Sage** is known to purify and enhance the ability to speak your truth confidently.

6. Third Eye Chakra (Ajna)

- **Herbs**: Mugwort, Eyebright, Gotu Kola, and Jasmine

- **Insight**: The Third Eye Chakra, located between the eyebrows, governs intuition, wisdom, and vision. Herbs that enhance mental clarity, intuition, and spiritual awareness are perfect for this chakra. **Mugwort tea** enhances dreams and intuition, making it an excellent choice for those looking to open their Third Eye. **Gotu Kola** helps improve mental clarity and focus, connecting you to deeper insight.

7. Crown Chakra (Sahasrara)

- **Herbs**: Holy Basil (Tulsi), Lavender, Lotus, and White Sage

- **Insight**: The Crown Chakra, located at the top of the head, is all about spiritual connection and enlightenment. Herbs that promote relaxation, clarity, and a connection to the divine are best for this chakra. **Holy Basil (Tulsi)** tea is known for its calming and spiritually uplifting properties, helping to align and open the Crown Chakra. **Lavender** soothes the mind and invites a sense of spiritual clarity and peace.

Herbal teas are a gentle yet powerful way to support the energy flow in your chakras. Mindfully choosing the right herbs can balance your body's energy centers while enjoying a calming daily ritual. Whether grounding with dandelion root or opening your intuition with mugwort, these herbs provide hydration, healing, and a deep connection to your energy.

Preparing herbal teas is a delightful ritual to enhance your chakra healing practice. Combine dandelion root and a pinch of cinnamon for a grounding Root Chakra tea in boiling water. Let it steep for about ten minutes before straining and sipping. The earthy flavors will help you feel more anchored and secure. For a Heart Chakra tea, blend hawthorn berries and rose petals. This fragrant, floral tea tastes divine and opens your heart to love and compassion.

Incorporating herbs into your daily rituals can be both simple and transformative. Consider starting your day with a cup of herbal tea that aligns with the chakra you wish to focus on. You can also use herbs in other ways, such as herbal baths. Imagine soaking in a warm bath infused with ashwagandha and rose petals, feeling the stress melt away as these herbs work their magic on your energy centers. Creating herbal sachets for your meditation space is another beautiful idea. Fill small fabric bags with herbs like peppermint and sage, and place them around your meditation area. The aroma will enhance your practice and help balance your chakras.

Herbs and teas offer a natural, accessible way to support your chakra health. Incorporating these botanical allies into your daily routine can enhance energy flow through your chakras and promote overall well-being. So, next time you brew a cup of herbal tea, take a moment to appreciate the ancient wisdom steeped in every sip.

Color Therapy: Using Colors to Influence Chakra Health

Imagine waking up on a dreary Monday morning, feeling like you're trudging through mud. Now, picture slipping on a bright red sweater and suddenly feeling a surge of energy and motivation. That's the magic of color therapy. Colors profoundly impact our mood and energy levels, and this ancient practice taps into that power to balance and heal our chakras. Color therapy, or chromotherapy, uses specific colors to influence our physical, emotional, and spiritual well-being. Historically, cultures like the Egyptians and Greeks believed in the healing power of colors, using them in various rituals and treatments. Modern color therapy builds on these ancient practices, focusing on how different colors can align and balance our chakras.

Each chakra resonates with a specific color, and incorporating these colors into your daily life can help maintain balance. ***The Root Chakra***, located at the base of your spine, resonates with the color red. This vibrant hue is all about grounding and stability. Wearing red clothing or incorporating red elements into your surroundings can help you feel more secure and anchored. The ***Sacral Chakra***, found in the lower abdomen, is associated with orange. This cheerful color stimulates creativity and pleasure. Think about adding orange accents to your workspace or wearing an orange scarf to boost your creative energy.

The ***Solar Plexus Chakra*** in your upper abdomen resonates with the color yellow. This sunny shade is linked to confidence and personal power.

Wearing yellow or surrounding yourself with yellow objects can help you feel more empowered and self-assured. Each chakra has its own unique color that influences specific aspects of your life, making color therapy a versatile and accessible tool for chakra healing.

There are several practical ways to incorporate color therapy into your daily life. One of the simplest methods is by wearing clothing in chakra-specific colors. If you feel ungrounded, use red attire to stabilize your Root Chakra. To boost your confidence, wear something yellow to invigorate your Solar Plexus Chakra. Another practical approach is using colored lighting in your living spaces. For instance, you can use orange lighting in your creative space to stimulate your Sacral Chakra or blue lighting in your study area to enhance communication and clarity associated with the Throat Chakra.

Here's a chart of the chakras and the corresponding colors used in color therapy:

Chakra	Location	Color
Root Chakra (Muladhara)	Base of the spine	Red
Sacral Chakra (Svadhisthana)	Lower abdomen	Orange
Solar Plexus Chakra (Manipura)	Above the navel	Yellow
Heart Chakra (Anahata)	Center of the chest	Green (or Pink)
Throat Chakra (Vishuddha)	Throat area	Blue
Third Eye Chakra (Ajna)	Between the eyebrows	Indigo (or Dark Blue)
Crown Chakra (Sahasrara)	Top of the head	Violet (or White)

This chart can be used as a reference for matching chakras with their associated colors in color therapy.

Visualization techniques focusing on chakra colors can also be incredibly powerful. Find a quiet space, close your eyes, and take a few deep breaths.

Visualize the specific color associated with the chakra you wish to balance. Imagine this color as a glowing light, enveloping the chakra and clearing blockages. Feel the energy of the color infusing your body, restoring balance and harmony. This practice can be done anytime, anywhere, and is a fantastic way to realign your energy quickly.

Various tools and accessories can enhance your color therapy practice. Chakra color charts are a handy reference, helping you quickly identify the colors associated with each chakra. You can find these charts online or create your personalized version. Colored meditation cushions are another great addition. Imagine sitting on a vibrant green cushion while meditating on your Heart Chakra, feeling your love and compassion radiate. Color therapy glasses are also available, allowing you to wear lenses in specific colors to enhance your chakra healing throughout the day.

Incorporating these tools into your routine makes it easier to engage with color therapy and reap its benefits. Whether wearing a red sweater to ground yourself or meditating on a green cushion to open your heart, these simple practices can significantly enhance your chakra healing journey. So, next time you feel out of balance, consider reaching for the colors of the rainbow to restore harmony and vitality.

DIY Chakra Healing Toolkit: Creating Your Healing Tools

Creating your chakra healing tools can be a deeply personal and rewarding experience. It is cost-effective and allows you to infuse your tools with personal intentions and energy, making them even more potent. Think of it as adding a touch of your unique essence to your healing practice. Plus, there's something incredibly satisfying about using items you've crafted yourself.

Let's start with making your chakra stones:

- First, gather some smooth, flat stones—river rocks work well. Clean them thoroughly. Next, select acrylic paints in the colors corresponding to each chakra: red for the Root, orange for the Sacral, yellow for the Solar Plexus, green for the Heart, blue for the Throat, indigo for the Third Eye, and violet for the Crown. Paint each stone with its respective color and let them dry. To infuse them with personal intentions, hold each stone in your hand, close your eyes, and focus on what you want to achieve with that chakra. For example, while holding the red stone, you might set an intention for grounding and stability.

- DIY essential oil blends are another fantastic addition to your healing toolkit. Mix Patchouli, Cedarwood, and Vetiver essential oils with a carrier oil like Jojoba for the Root Chakra. This blend promotes grounding and security. For the Sacral Chakra, combine Orange, Ylang Ylang, and Sandalwood. This mixture enhances creativity and emotional balance. To create these blends, use a small glass bottle, add a few drops of each essential oil, and top it off with the carrier oil. Shake well and store in a cool, dark place. Apply these blends to the corresponding chakra points or use them in a diffuser during meditation.

- Crafting chakra bracelets can be a fun and meaningful project. Select beads in colors that correspond to each chakra. You can use gemstones like Red Jasper for the Root or Amethyst for the Crown or choose beads in the appropriate colors. Start by measuring your wrist and cutting a piece of elastic cord slightly longer than that measurement. String the beads onto the cord, arranging them in the order of the chakras from Root to Crown. Once all the beads are on, tie a secure knot and trim any excess cord. Wear this bracelet as a reminder of your balanced energy centers.

- Making personalized meditation cushions is another way to enhance your chakra healing practice. Start by selecting fabrics in the colors of the chakras. You might choose a soft green for the Heart Chakra or a calming blue for the Throat Chakra. Cut the fabric into two square pieces, sew three sides together, and stuff it with filling. Before sewing the final side, add a few drops of essential oil to the stuffing. This infuses the cushion with the healing properties of the oils. Sew up the last side, and you have a custom meditation cushion that supports your chakra work.

These DIY projects make your healing tools more personal and allow you to engage with your chakras hands-only. Each time you use a stone you've painted, an oil blend you've mixed, a bracelet you've strung, or a cushion you've sewn, you're connecting with your energy centers on a deeper level. Plus, the process of creating these items can be meditative and healing in itself.

Creating Personalized Affirmation Cards

Imagine waking up daily to a positive affirmation setting your day's tone. Affirmation cards can be a powerful tool for chakra healing and personal growth. These cards are daily reminders of your intentions and goals, providing positive reinforcement for energy balance. Focusing on specific affirmations can align your thoughts and actions with your desired outcomes, promoting well-being and balance. It's like having a little pep talk with yourself, tailored to support your unique journey.

To create your personalized affirmation cards, you'll need some basic supplies. Start with blank cards or cardstock, which you can find at any craft store. You'll also need markers, pens, or paints to add color and creativity to your cards. Consider gathering some inspirational quotes or personal affirmations that resonate with you. These can come from books, online sources, or your own heart. The goal is to create cards that speak to you and support your chakra healing practice.

Crafting affirmation cards is a fun and meditative process. Begin by setting aside some quiet time where you won't be disturbed. Choose a comfortable space with calming music or a diffuser with your favorite essential oil. Start by selecting or creating an affirmation for each chakra. Below are more in-depth ideas to help you with your affirmations.

- For the Root Chakra, you might write, "I am grounded and secure." For the Sacral Chakra, "I embrace my creativity and passions" can be a powerful affirmation. For the Solar Plexus Chakra, try "I am confident and empowered," while "I trust my intuition and inner wisdom" can be profoundly affirming for the Third Eye Chakra.

- Once you have your affirmations, it's time to design your cards. Use your markers, pens, or paints to decorate a blank card. You can add colors corresponding to each chakra, such as red for the Root Chakra or indigo for the Third Eye Chakra. Write your affirmation clearly on the card, making it easy to read. You might also want to add some embellishments, like stickers or drawings, to make the cards more personal and visually appealing.

- Organize your cards in a way that is easy to use. You can keep them in a small box or a decorative pouch, placing them in an order that aligns with the chakras. This way, you can easily pull out the card you need for daily inspiration or meditation. You might also consider creating a display where you can see your affirmations regularly, such as on a vision board or a dedicated space on your desk.

- Affirmation cards are not just pretty pieces of paper but tools for transformation. Regular use can reinforce positive beliefs and intentions, helping shift your mindset and energy. Start your day by selecting a card and reading the affirmation aloud. Take a few moments to breathe deeply and let the words resonate with you. Throughout the day, revisit the affirmation, especially during moments of stress or doubt. This simple practice can align you with your goals and maintain balanced energy.

- Creating and using affirmation cards can be a deeply personal and empowering practice. It's a way to take charge of your energy and intentions, providing daily support for your chakra healing journey. So gather your supplies, set your intentions, and start crafting your personalized affirmation cards. Each card will be a testament to your commitment to growth and balance, a small but powerful tool in your healing toolkit.

Introduction to Chakra Affirmations

Affirmations are powerful tools to enhance your chakra healing journey by aligning your energy centers with positive intentions. Repeating these affirmations with focus and belief can help release blockages, promote balance, and strengthen each chakra. Whether spoken aloud, written down, or meditated on, these affirmations allow you to connect more deeply with yourself and the energy flowing through your body.

Below are examples of affirmations for each chakra. Use these to guide your practice, empowering you to cultivate strength, creativity, love, clarity, and spiritual connection.

Root Chakra (Muladhara)

- "I am deeply rooted, supported, and at peace with my place in the world."

- "I trust the process of life and feel safe in my body."

- "I am grounded, secure, and stable in everything I do."

Sacral Chakra (Svadhisthana)

1. "I honor my emotions and embrace life's creative energy flow."

2. "I deserve pleasure, joy, and fulfillment in all areas of my life."

3. "I am passionate, vibrant, and open to experiencing life fully."

Solar Plexus Chakra (Manipura)

1. "I am empowered, confident, and in control of my power."

2. "I trust myself and my ability to take bold, decisive actions."

3. "I am worthy of success and easily manifest my goals."

Heart Chakra (Anahata)

1. "I open my heart to love, forgiveness, and compassion for myself and others."

2. "I deserve unconditional love, and I radiate peace and kindness."

3. "I forgive myself and others, creating space for love and harmony in my life."

Throat Chakra (Vishuddha)

1. "I speak my truth with clarity, courage, and confidence."

2. "My voice matters, and I express myself openly and honestly."

3. "I listen to others respectfully and am heard in return."

Third Eye Chakra (Ajna)

1. "I trust my intuition and see the path ahead clearly."

2. "I am in tune with my inner wisdom and open to divine guidance."

3. "My mind is clear, and I trust my insights to guide me in the right direction."

Crown Chakra (Sahasrara)

1. "I am connected to the infinite wisdom of the universe and my higher self."

2. "I trust in the divine timing of my life, and I am aligned with my purpose."

3. "I am open to spiritual growth and the unfolding of my soul's journey."

These affirmations are potent tools for focusing and aligning with each chakra, promoting balance and harmony along your spiritual path.

Incorporating Chakras into Daily Rituals: Practical Applications

Have you ever noticed how some days start tremendously and keep improving? That's the power of a good morning ritual. Incorporating chakras into your daily rituals can promote consistency and mindfulness, making every day feel like a good start. When you set aside time each day to focus on your chakras, you enhance your overall well-being. Let's face it: Life gets busy, and it's easy to overlook self-care. But making chakra work part of your routine can help you stay balanced and grounded, even on the busiest days.

Morning rituals are particularly effective for setting the tone for the day. For the Root Chakra, start with grounding exercises and affirmations. As soon as you wake up, take a moment to sit on the edge of your bed with your feet firmly planted on the ground. Close your eyes and take a few deep breaths. Visualize roots growing from your feet into the earth, grounding and stabilizing you. Repeat affirmations like, "I am grounded and secure." This simple act can help you feel more anchored and ready to face the day. Follow this with a Sun Salutation yoga sequence to energize your Solar Plexus Chakra. This sequence involves a series of poses that flow smoothly from one to the next, helping to awaken your body and ignite your power.

Evening rituals are as important for winding down and preparing for restful sleep. For the Heart Chakra, try gratitude journaling. Before bed, take a few minutes to write down three things you're grateful for. This practice shifts your focus from any stress or negativity to the positive aspects of your day, opening your heart to love and compassion. For the Throat Chakra, engage in reflective meditation and mantra chanting. Sit in a quiet space, close your eyes, and take a few deep breaths. Reflect on your day, paying attention to moments where you expressed yourself well or struggled to communicate. Chant a mantra like "HAM," focusing on the vibrations in your throat. This practice can help clear any blockages and promote better communication.

Integrating chakra awareness into daily activities can be both simple and transformative. Consider mindful eating as a way to support your chakras. Choose foods that align with specific chakras, like root vegetables for the Root Chakra or leafy greens for the Heart Chakra. As you eat, focus on the colors, textures, and flavors, savoring each bite. This mindful approach nourishes your body and balances your energy centers. Another effective method is using chakra-related affirmations throughout the day. If you're anxious, repeat a Root Chakra affirmation like, "I am safe and secure." If you need a confidence boost, try a Solar Plexus Chakra affirmation like, "I am powerful and capable." These small, intentional acts can make a big difference in your feelings.

Incorporating chakras into your daily rituals doesn't have to be complicated or time-consuming. It's about making small, intentional choices that support your well-being. Whether you're grounding yourself first thing in the morning, expressing gratitude before bed, or practicing mindful eating, these rituals can help you stay balanced and connected to your energy centers. Making chakra work a part of your daily routine makes it easier to navigate life's ups and downs with grace and resilience.

Enhancing Your Space: Feng Shui and Chakra Alignment

Have you ever walked into a room and felt an instant sense of calm or, conversely, a wave of unease? That's the impact of your environment on your energy. Feng Shui, an ancient Chinese practice, revolves around the idea that the arrangement of your space can influence the flow of energy within it. This concept aligns perfectly with chakra healing, as both focus on balancing energy to promote well-being. Feng Shui aims to create harmony between individuals and their environment, ensuring that power, or "chi," flows smoothly. When applied to chakra alignment, this means arranging your living space to support the balance and health of your energy centers.

Creating a chakra-aligned space begins with understanding the role of your environment in chakra health. Each room in your home can be tailored to support specific chakras, enhancing the overall energy flow. Incorporating earth elements like plants and natural stones can be incredibly effective for the Root Chakra, which is all about grounding and stability. Imagine a cozy corner filled with lush greenery and grounded by a few well-placed stones—this setup fosters a sense of security and connection to the earth.

The Heart Chakra thrives in a space filled with softness and warmth. Think about using inviting furniture and decor that emanates comfort and love. Soft cushions, plush throws, and even artwork that evokes feelings of compassion can help open and balance your Heart Chakra. Picture a living room where every piece of furniture invites you to sit, relax, and connect with your loved ones—this environment nurtures your heart center.

Color plays a crucial role in both Feng Shui and chakra healing. Calming colors like deep blues and indigos can enhance intuition and inner wisdom for the Third Eye Chakra. Consider using these colors in your bedding and curtains to create a tranquil atmosphere conducive to deep thought and meditation. On the other hand, the Sacral Chakra, which governs creativity and pleasure, benefits from stimulating colors like vibrant oranges. Incorporating orange accents in your artwork or wall colors can invigorate this energy center, sparking creativity and joy.

Enhancing your space for chakra work involves creating dedicated sacred spaces. A meditation corner, for example, can be a powerful addition to your home. Fill this space with items that resonate with your chakras, such as specific crystals, candles, and symbolic objects. Imagine a serene corner with a comfortable cushion surrounded by items that ground you, open your heart, or enhance your intuition. This becomes your go-to spot for meditation and reflection, a sanctuary for energy work.

An altar is another beautiful way to enhance your space. This doesn't have to be elaborate; a simple setup with a few meaningful items can be incredibly powerful. Place crystals corresponding to the chakras you're focusing on, light a candle to symbolize illumination, and add any other objects that hold significance. This altar becomes a focal point for your intentions and energy work, anchoring your practice in a physical space.

Incorporating Feng Shui principles into your chakra healing practice can create a harmonious environment supporting your well-being. By thoughtfully arranging your space and using colors, textures, and meaningful objects, you can enhance the flow of energy in your home and within yourself. So, look around your living space and consider how to make small changes to support your chakra health. Even minor adjustments can significantly impact your energy, helping you feel more balanced and aligned.

By blending the ancient wisdom of Feng Shui with the principles of chakra healing, you create a living environment that supports your journey toward balance and harmony. Whether incorporating earth elements for grounding or using calming colors to enhance intuition, these practices offer practical ways to align your space with your energy centers.

Chapter 4:
Emotional and Spiritual Healing

One rainy afternoon, I found myself staring at an old photo album. As I flipped through the pages, a wave of emotions washed over me. Joy, nostalgia, and then, out of nowhere, a deep sadness. It was like opening a Pandora's box of feelings I didn't even know I had. That moment was a revelation. I realized that my emotional baggage wasn't just in my mind—it was stored in my body, affecting my energy centers. This was my first encounter with emotional blockages, and it set me on a path to understanding how trauma can get stuck in our chakras and what we can do to release it.

Emotional Blockages: Identifying and Releasing Trauma

Emotional blockages are like invisible knots in your energy centers, disrupting the natural flow of energy and causing various issues. Think of your chakras as vortexes of electromagnetic energy that give and receive energy. When emotional wounds or trauma block these vortexes, they prevent the delivery of prana (life force) to the body, leading to stress, anxiety, and tension. Trauma can be stored in the body in various ways, affecting your mind and physical health. This stored trauma can manifest as tightness, pain, or discomfort in specific areas, depending on which chakra is affected.

Identifying these blockages is the first step toward healing. Physical symptoms are often the most noticeable. You might experience tightness in your chest, indicating a blocked Heart Chakra, or a persistent lump in your throat, pointing to issues with your Throat Chakra. Emotional symptoms can be just as telling. Anxiety, depression, and anger are common signs that your chakras might be out of balance. Behavioral symptoms like avoidance, overreaction, or withdrawal can also indicate emotional blockages. If you find yourself dodging social interactions or snapping at loved ones for no apparent reason, it might be worth exploring which chakras are affected.

Releasing trauma and emotional blockages requires a multifaceted approach. Somatic experiencing is one effective technique. This involves focusing on physical sensations in your body to release stored trauma. Paying attention to where you feel tightness or discomfort can unravel these knots and allow energy to flow freely again. Another powerful method is Emotional Freedom Techniques (EFT), also known as tapping. EFT combines psychotherapy with acupressure, tapping specific meridian points on the body while acknowledging your emotions. This helps to process and transform these emotions, creating new neural pathways in the brain and regulating the nervous system. Expressive arts therapy is another avenue to explore. Art, dance, or music to express and release emotions can be incredibly therapeutic. These creative outlets allow you to bypass the logical mind and access deeper layers of emotion, facilitating healing.

Let me share a story about a friend named Sarah. Sarah had struggled with anxiety for years, a lingering shadow from a difficult childhood. Traditional therapy helped, but it wasn't until she started working with her chakras that she experienced a significant shift. By focusing on her Root and Heart Chakras and combining somatic experiencing and EFT, Sarah began to feel more grounded and open. She'd tap on meridian points, saying, *"Even though I feel this anxiety in my chest, I love and accept myself."* Over time, her anxiety lessened, and she felt more balanced and at peace.

Another example is John, who used EFT to reduce his anxiety and restore balance. John found that tapping on specific points—like the side of the hand and under the eye—while acknowledging his feelings of stress helped him process these emotions more effectively. He'd say, *"Even though I feel this stress in my stomach, I deeply and completely accept myself."* This simple yet powerful practice made a noticeable difference in his emotional and physical well-being.

Incorporating these techniques into your daily routine can help you release emotional blockages and restore balance to your chakras. Whether focusing on physical sensations, tapping on meridian points, or expressing yourself through art, these methods offer practical ways to address and heal stored trauma. Understanding and working through these emotional blocks allows you to experience greater wisdom, empathy, and a more centered presence.

Emotional Freedom Techniques (EFT)

I've mentioned EFT, or tapping, a few times already, but now it's time to dig deeper into what it is and how it can be a powerful tool for balancing our chakras. It's one of those practices that seems so simple on the surface yet has the potential to unlock so much emotional and energetic healing.

Emotional Freedom Techniques, or tapping, is a therapeutic practice that blends cognitive therapy, exposure therapy, and acupressure—all through tapping on specific points along the body's meridian lines. These are the same meridians referenced in Traditional Chinese Medicine (TCM), and the more I explored EFT, the more I realized how closely this technique aligns with chakra healing. Tapping into these meridian points allows us to connect with the body's energy system, like working with the chakras. It offers a way to clear emotional blockages and restore harmony.

In practice, EFT is deceptively simple. You tap on key points like the top of the head, which corresponds with the Crown Chakra, or around the eyes, linked to the Third Eye Chakra. As you move down the body—tapping under the nose, on the chin (the Throat Chakra), and along the collarbone (the Heart Chakra)—you're not just tapping into physical points. You're engaging with your energy centers. It's incredible how these points mirror the locations of our chakras, each holding a layer of emotional or spiritual meaning. And while you tap, you affirm, "Even though I feel this fear, I deeply and completely accept myself." These words are like a soft release, acknowledging the discomfort while inviting in healing—much like chakra work itself.

The benefits of EFT are undeniable. Studies have shown how effective tapping can be in reducing stress, anxiety, and even the lingering shadows of PTSD. As I explored EFT, it became clear that it's similar to chakra balancing, especially when discussing how emotional or physical issues can arise from blocked energy centers. Tapping clears the "mental clutter," just as opening your chakras can invite clarity and light into areas where we feel stuck. It's like pressing a reset button on your internal system, allowing energy to flow freely again—through your body, mind, and spirit.

What I love most about EFT is how it strengthens the mind-body-spirit connection. Taping on the Crown Chakra may make you feel more connected to your spiritual self. Or, when you tap on the Heart Chakra, you might feel an emotional release—a softening, a more profound compassion for yourself or others. In these moments, tapping feels like more than just a technique; it feels like a spiritual practice—a way to reconnect to parts of yourself that may have felt distant or blocked off.

Even science is beginning to catch up to what many practitioners have known for a long time. Research suggests that EFT helps stimulate the brain's limbic system, which is responsible for emotions and stress responses. It calms the body's threat response and shifts us into a more relaxed, healing state, similar to when you balance your chakras. Tapping, much like energy healing, engages the parasympathetic nervous system, helping us move into "rest and digest" mode, where true healing can take place.

Ultimately, EFT is a holistic healing tool that mirrors the principles of chakra work. It's a gentle yet powerful way to align the emotional, physical, and spiritual aspects of ourselves, and it's one that I believe can offer profound benefits for anyone willing to give it a try.

This black-and-white diagram illustrates the primary meridian points used in Emotional Freedom Techniques (EFT), also known as tapping. The image displays a front-facing human body with specific tapping points clearly labeled, including:

- **Top of the Head (Crown Chakra)**: This point is associated with spiritual awareness and connection.

- **Eyebrow (Third Eye Chakra)**: Located just above the brow, this point is linked to intuition and insight.

- **Side of the Eye**: This meridian point helps address emotions like anger and frustration.

- **Under the Eye**: Connected to fear and anxiety, this point relates to feelings of safety.

- **Under the Nose**: A key point for releasing guilt and shame.

- **Chin (Throat Chakra)**: This point is associated with self-expression and communication.

- **Collarbone (Heart Chakra)**: Tapping here helps balance emotions related to love, compassion, and grief.

- **Under the Arm**: Tied to the Root Chakra, this point aids in releasing feelings of insecurity and fear related to safety and grounding.

This simple, easy-to-understand diagram provides a visual guide for tapping into chakra alignment and emotional healing practices.

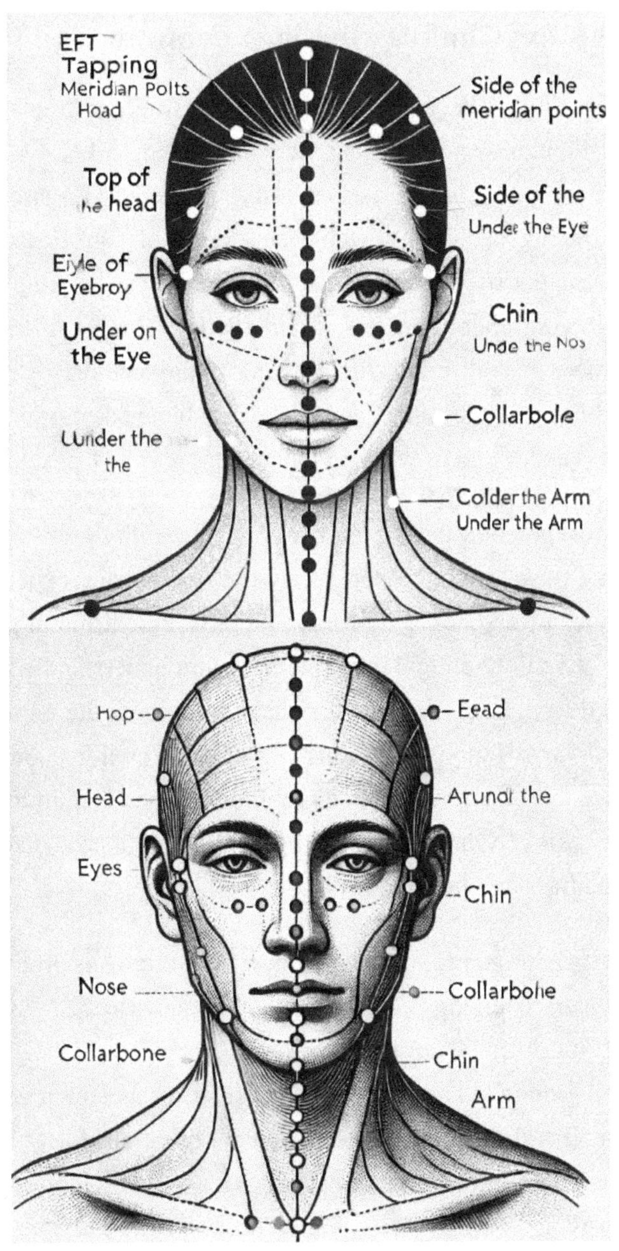

EFT
Tapping
Meridian Points
Head
Top of
the head
Eije of
Eyebroy
Under on
the Eye
Under the
the
Side of the
meridian points
Side of the
Under the Eye
Chin
Under the Nos
Collarbole
Colder the Arm
Under the Arm
Hop
Head
Eyes
Nose
Collarbone
Eead
Arund the
Chin
Collarbohe
Chin
Arm

Journaling for Chakra Healing: Prompts and Practices

Journaling has always been my go-to whenever I needed to make sense of my swirling thoughts and emotions. It's like having a heart-to-heart with yourself, where you can be sincere and unfiltered. Regarding chakra healing, journaling takes on a whole new level of significance. Writing things down can clarify your emotions and experiences, making identifying imbalances in your energy centers easier. It's like shining a flashlight into the dark corners of your mind, illuminating things you didn't even realize were there. Putting pen to paper can help release blocked emotions, allowing you to process and let go of what no longer serves you.

One of the most potent aspects of journaling is its ability to foster emotional clarity and self-awareness. When you write about your experiences and feelings, you can step back and observe them from a different perspective. This can be incredibly enlightening, helping you understand why you feel the way you do and how certain events have impacted your energy centers. For instance, if you find yourself constantly feeling anxious, journaling can help you trace this anxiety back to its root, often revealing an imbalance in your Root Chakra. By bringing these hidden emotions to the surface, you can start to address and heal them.

Chakra-specific journal prompts can guide you through this process, helping you focus on each energy center and its unique aspects. For the **Root Chakra**, ask yourself, *"What makes you feel safe and secure?"* Reflect on when you felt grounded and stable, and consider what elements contributed to that feeling. For the **Sacral Chakra**, explore questions like, *"How do you express your creativity and sexuality?"* Think about how you channel your creative energy and connect with your sensuality. For the **Heart Chakra**, delve into *"What are your experiences with giving and receiving love?"* Reflect on your relationships and how you show and accept love. These prompts can open doors to deeper understanding and healing.

Establishing a consistent journaling practice is critical to reaping its benefits. Find a time and space that works for you, whether first thing in the morning, during lunch, or before bed. The important thing is to make it a routine. Set an intention for each journaling session. Maybe you want to explore a specific emotion or focus on a particular chakra. A clear intention can guide your writing and make the practice more meaningful. Don't worry about grammar or spelling—this is for your eyes only. Let your thoughts flow freely, and don't censor yourself. The more honest and rawer you are, the more influential the practice will be.

Combining journaling with other chakra healing practices can amplify its effects. Consider using essential oils or candles during your journaling sessions. For instance, diffuse lavender oil to promote relaxation or light a candle to create a calming atmosphere. These sensory elements can enhance your focus and deepen your connection to your energy centers. Another powerful combination is journaling and meditation. Start with a brief meditation to center yourself and connect with your chakras, then move into your journaling practice. This can help you tap into deeper subconscious layers, bringing hidden emotions and insights to the surface.

Guided Visualizations: Healing Emotional Wounds

Imagine closing your eyes and finding yourself in a serene forest, the sunlight filtering through the leaves and a gentle breeze brushing against your face. This is the power of guided visualization, a technique that can profoundly impact your emotional well-being and balance your chakras. Guided visualization involves using mental imagery to create a healing environment, facilitating emotional healing, and aligning your energy centers. It's like giving your mind a mini-vacation, allowing it to explore soothing landscapes and scenarios that promote relaxation and balance.

To understand how guided visualizations can help, consider this: Your mind doesn't always distinguish between real and imagined experiences. When you visualize a calming scene, your body responds as if you were there, reducing stress and promoting a sense of peace. This technique can be particularly effective for balancing chakras, as each energy center can be associated with specific visualizations that help clear blockages and restore harmony. For example, visualizing a safe, grounding place can help balance the Root Chakra, while imagining a green light expanding from your heart can heal the Heart Chakra.

Let's start with a visualization for the **Root Chakra:**

- Picture yourself in a place where you feel completely safe and secure, like a cozy cabin in the woods or a warm, sandy beach. Imagine the solid and supportive ground beneath you, anchoring you. Feel the stability and strength this connection to the earth provides. This visualization can help release fear and anxiety, grounding you and bringing balance to your Root Chakra.

- For the **Heart Chakra,** visualize a vibrant green light in the center of your chest. Imagine this light growing brighter and expanding outward with each breath, filling your entire body with warmth and love. This visualization can help heal emotional wounds and open your heart to compassion and self-love.

- For the **Crown Chakra,** which connects you to higher consciousness, try envisioning a connection to a higher source of wisdom. Picture a white or violet light pouring into the top of your head, filling you with a sense of peace and spiritual connection. Feel this light expanding, connecting you to the universe and enhancing your spiritual awareness. This visualization can help you feel more connected to something greater than yourself, promoting unity and enlightenment.

Creating a conducive environment for guided visualizations is vital to maximizing their benefits. Choose a quiet, comfortable space where you won't be disturbed. Soft lighting can create a calming atmosphere, and soothing background music can help you relax and focus. The goal is to create a safe and inviting space, allowing you to immerse yourself fully in the visualization.

Guided Visualization Script: Releasing Fear and Anxiety from the Root Chakra

Find a quiet place and sit comfortably. Close your eyes and take a few deep breaths. Imagine yourself in a safe, grounding place, like a forest or a beach. Feel the ground beneath you, solid and supportive. Visualize roots growing from your feet into the earth, anchoring you. With each breath, feel the stability and strength this connection provides. As you exhale, release any fear or anxiety, letting it flow into the earth. Continue breathing deeply, feeling more grounded and secure with each breath.

Another powerful visualization for healing heartbreak and fostering self-love involves focusing on the Heart Chakra. Close your eyes and take a deep breath. Visualize a green light in the center of your chest, growing brighter with each inhale. Imagine it filling your body with warmth and love as the light expands. Think of someone or something you love deeply, and let that feeling of love radiate outward. As you exhale, release any pain or hurt, letting it dissolve into the green light. Continue this visualization, feeling your heart open and filled with love and compassion.

Guided visualizations offer a gentle yet powerful way to balance chakras and heal emotional wounds. You can promote emotional and spiritual well-being by creating a safe space and using specific visualizations tailored to each chakra. Whether you're visualizing a safe, grounding place, a vibrant green light, or a connection to higher wisdom, these techniques can help you feel more balanced, peaceful, and connected.

Intuition and the Third Eye Chakra: Unlocking Inner Wisdom

Sitting quietly, I often find myself drawn to the space between my eyebrows, the area known as the Third Eye Chakra. This energy center, located right in the middle of your forehead, is your gateway to intuition, insight, and clarity. The Third Eye Chakra, also called Ajna in Sanskrit, is like your internal GPS, guiding you through life's twists and turns. When it's open and balanced, you can tap into your inner wisdom, see the bigger picture, and confidently make decisions. But when it's blocked, you might feel lost, confused, or disconnected from your true self.

Mindfulness meditation is a fantastic starting point to enhance your intuition and strengthen the Third Eye Chakra. Find a quiet spot, close your eyes, and focus on your breath. Allow your thoughts to come and go without judgment. This practice helps clear the mental clutter, making it easier to hear your inner voice. Another effective technique is dream journaling. Keep a notebook by your bed and jot down your dreams as soon as you wake up. Dreams are a window into your subconscious, offering valuable insights and guidance. You can uncover hidden messages and enhance your intuition by recording and interpreting them.

Intuitive exercises can also be incredibly beneficial. Try practicing with oracle cards or a pendulum. Oracle cards are a fun way to tap into your intuition. Shuffle the deck, ask a question, and draw a card. Pay attention to the imagery and how it makes you feel. Trust your initial impressions—they often hold the most truth. Using a pendulum is another excellent method. Hold the pendulum steady and ask yes or no questions. Observe its movements and trust the answers you receive. These tools can help you build confidence in your intuitive abilities and strengthen your Third Eye Chakra.

Recognizing and trusting your intuitive messages is crucial. Intuitive guidance often comes in subtle forms, like gut feelings, synchronicities, or sudden insights. A gut feeling might be a physical sensation in your stomach, guiding you toward or away from something. Synchronicities are meaningful coincidences that seem too perfect to be random, like running into an old friend when you needed their advice. Sudden insights are those "aha" moments where everything clicks into place. Differentiating between intuition and fear-based thoughts can be tricky. Fear-based thoughts are usually accompanied by anxiety or a sense of urgency, while intuitive messages feel calm and clear. Trust the quiet voice—it's your intuition speaking.

Let me share a story about my friend, Emma. Emma had always been curious about her intuitive abilities but unsure how to develop them. She started with mindfulness meditation, spending just ten minutes each morning focusing on her breath. Over time, she noticed that her mind felt clearer and began to trust her gut feelings more. Encouraged by this progress, Emma started using oracle cards. She'd draw a card each day and reflect on its meaning. One day, she pulled a card encouraging her to leap of faith. That same week, she received an unexpected job offer. Trusting her intuition, she accepted the offer, which was a perfect fit, leading to greater career satisfaction and personal growth.

Another example is James, who used dream journaling to enhance his intuition. James had vivid dreams but never paid much attention to them. After learning about the Third Eye Chakra, he started a dream journal. Each morning, he'd jot down his dreams and look for patterns. One recurring dream involved a bridge, which he eventually realized symbolized the need to connect two aspects of his life—work and passion. This insight led him to pursue a side project that combined his professional skills with his love for music. The project brought him joy and opened new opportunities he hadn't considered before.

Intuition is like a muscle—the more you use it, the stronger it becomes. By practicing mindfulness, recording your dreams, and using intuitive tools like oracle cards or a pendulum, you can enhance your Third Eye Chakra and unlock your inner wisdom. Recognizing and trusting your intuitive messages can guide you toward positive changes and deeper self-awareness. Your intuition is a powerful ally whether you're making decisions, seeking clarity, or simply exploring your inner world. Trust it, nurture it, and let it give you greater insight and clarity.

Heart Chakra Healing: Cultivating Love and Compassion

You know that warm, fuzzy feeling when you hug a loved one or see a touching scene in a movie? That's your Heart Chakra at work. Nestled right in the center of your chest, the Heart Chakra, or Anahata, is the fourth chakra in the body's energy system. It acts as a bridge between the lower and upper chakras, connecting the physical with the spiritual. This chakra is all about love, compassion, and emotional balance. You feel open, loving, and empathetic when it's in harmony. When it's blocked, you might experience loneliness, bitterness, or even physical issues like heart problems or respiratory conditions. Cultivating a balanced Heart Chakra can transform your relationships and emotional well-being, making life more prosperous and connected.

Healing the Heart Chakra involves a variety of practices that open and balance this vital energy center. One effective technique is loving-kindness meditation. Sit comfortably, close your eyes, and take a few deep breaths. Begin by sending love and compassion to yourself. Repeat phrases like, "May I be happy. May I be healthy? May I be at peace." Then, gradually extend these wishes to others, starting with loved ones and eventually including those you find challenging. This practice opens your heart and fosters empathy and compassion for others. Heart-opening yoga poses are another powerful tool. Camel Pose (Ustrasana) involves kneeling and arching your back, reaching for your heels, which opens up the chest and heart area. Cobra Pose (Bhujangasana), where you lie on your stomach and lift your chest, also promotes heart chakra healing by expanding the chest and improving circulation.

Practicing gratitude can also work wonders for your Heart Chakra. Keeping a gratitude journal helps shift your focus from what's lacking to what you have, opening your heart to love and appreciation. Each day, jot down a few things you're grateful for—big or small. This simple act can elevate your mood and create a positive feedback loop, attracting more things for which you can be grateful. Over time, you'll notice a significant shift in your emotional state, making you more open and loving.

Addressing and healing emotional wounds related to the Heart Chakra often requires forgiveness exercises. Writing letters of forgiveness can be incredibly cathartic. Even if you don't send them, the act of writing helps release pent-up emotions and facilitates healing. Start by addressing the person you wish to forgive, explain how their actions affected you, and then express your intention to let go of the hurt. This process can be freeing and help you move forward with a lighter heart. Self-compassion practices are equally important. Use self-soothing techniques like placing your hand over your heart and repeating affirmations such as, "I am worthy of love and compassion." These practices can help you build a more loving relationship with yourself, which is the foundation for healthy relationships with others.

Let me tell you about Lisa, a friend who struggled with heartbreak after a difficult breakup. She felt closed off and unable to trust again. Through Heart Chakra healing, she began to transform. Lisa started with loving-kindness meditation, which helped her slowly open her heart to herself and others. She also kept a gratitude journal, focusing on positive aspects of her life. One significant step was writing a letter of forgiveness to her ex, which she never sent but felt immense relief after writing. These practices helped Lisa heal her emotional wounds and foster self-love. As a result, she became more open to new relationships and formed more profound connections with friends and family.

Another example is Mark, who used gratitude to enhance his emotional well-being. Mark had always been a bit of a cynic, finding it hard to see the positive side of things. He started a gratitude journal, writing down three daily things he was grateful for. At first, it felt forced, but it became a cherished ritual over time. This simple practice shifted his perspective, helping him see the good in his life and others. Mark found that he was happier and more optimistic, and his relationships improved.

Healing the Heart Chakra can transform your emotional and spiritual health, making you more open, loving, and compassionate. Whether through loving-kindness meditation, heart-opening yoga poses, gratitude practices, or forgiveness exercises, these techniques offer practical ways to balance this vital energy center. Nurturing your heart chakra can cultivate deeper connections and a more fulfilling emotional life.

The Crown Chakra: Connecting to Higher Consciousness

The Crown Chakra, also known as Sahasrara, is perched right at the top of your head. Think of it as your very own antenna to the universe. This chakra is your connection to higher consciousness, spiritual awareness, and enlightenment. Balancing is like having a clear, unobstructed view of the vast sky—a feeling of unity, profound peace, and an unshakable sense of purpose. The Crown Chakra isn't tied to any physical element, unlike the other chakras. Instead, it's all about pure consciousness, transcending the material world and connecting you to the divine.

Activating and balancing the Crown Chakra can be a transformative experience. One powerful technique is meditation for spiritual connection. Find a quiet place, sit comfortably, and close your eyes. Visualize a brilliant white or violet light pouring into the top of your head, filling your entire being. This light represents divine energy, bringing clarity and enlightenment. Chanting mantras can also be incredibly effective. The sound *"OM,"* often considered the universal sound, resonates deeply with the Crown Chakra. Chanting *"OM"* creates vibrations that align your energy with higher consciousness, fostering a sense of unity and peace. Contemplative practices, such as reflecting on spiritual texts or teachings, can further enhance your connection. Reading wisdom literature or contemplating the words of spiritual leaders can open your mind to new insights and deeper understanding.

Connecting with higher consciousness often brings about a profound shift in your perception of life. Signs of spiritual awakening can include increased intuition, a sense of unity with all beings, and a deep, abiding peace. You might notice that your intuition becomes sharper, guiding you with a clear inner voice. You may also experience moments of profound clarity, where everything seems interconnected, and you feel a deep sense of oneness with the universe. Integrating these spiritual insights into your daily life can be incredibly rewarding. Simple practices like mindfulness and gratitude can help you stay connected to this higher awareness. You can maintain this sense of peace and purpose by acknowledging the divine in everyday moments.

Let me share a story about a dear friend, Michael. Michael had always been spiritually curious but felt disconnected from any higher purpose. He decided to explore the Crown Chakra through meditation. Each morning, he would sit quietly, visualizing a white light entering the top of his head, filling him with divine energy. Over time, Michael noticed a shift. He felt more at peace, his intuition became sharper, and he experienced a deep sense of unity with the world around him. One day, during a particularly intense meditation, he felt a profound connection to the universe, as if he were part of something much more significant. This experience was transformative, leading him to pursue a more spiritual path and find deeper meaning in his life.

Another example is Laura, who found enlightenment through chanting "OM." Laura had always felt a sense of restlessness, a yearning for something more. She began incorporating the chant into her daily routine, focusing on the vibrations and the connection to the Crown Chakra. As she continued this practice, Laura experienced moments of profound clarity and peace. She felt a deep connection to the divine and a sense of purpose that had eluded her for years. This newfound spiritual awareness transformed her outlook on life, helping her navigate challenges gracefully and find joy in everyday moments.

Awakening the Crown Chakra can be a life-changing experience, opening the door to higher consciousness and spiritual enlightenment. Whether through meditation, chanting, or contemplative practices, these techniques offer powerful ways to connect with the divine and integrate spiritual insights into your daily life. You can experience a profound sense of peace, unity, and purpose by nurturing your Crown Chakra.

By now, you've discovered how emotional and spiritual healing can transform your life, from releasing emotional blockages to connecting with higher consciousness. Each practice, whether journaling, visualization, or meditation, contributes to a more balanced and harmonious existence. As you continue this journey, remember that every step you take brings you closer to understanding and healing your energy centers.

As we bring this chapter to a close, I know we've covered a lot of ground—tools, techniques, and insights to help you on your healing journey. To make things easier, here's a quick reference of the key takeaways to keep with you. Right after, you'll find a simple chart for tapping, mantras, and affirmations to guide you as you move forward in your practice.

1. **Emotional Blockages and Chakras**: Emotional trauma can get trapped in our energy centers, leading to physical symptoms like pain and discomfort or emotional disturbances like anxiety,

depression, or anger. Identifying and releasing these blockages is the first step to healing.

2. **EFT (Emotional Freedom Techniques)**: Tapping on specific meridian points while acknowledging your emotions is a powerful way to clear emotional blockages and restore energy flow through the chakras. This practice combines psychotherapy with acupressure to promote mental, physical, and spiritual healing.

3. **Somatic and Expressive Healing**: Techniques like somatic experiencing, where you focus on physical sensations, and expressive arts therapy, where you use creativity to release emotions, can help unblock the chakras and promote healing.

4. **Journaling for Clarity**: Journaling is a reflective practice that helps bring clarity to emotional experiences and uncover hidden imbalances in the chakras. Chakra-specific prompts can guide your self-exploration and emotional healing journey.

5. **Guided Visualizations and Chakra Healing**: Visualizing specific imagery or colors associated with each chakra can help balance your energy centers. This practice allows you to heal emotional wounds, cultivate compassion, and connect with higher spiritual awareness.

Quick Reference Chart for Chakra Affirmations and Tapping Chants

Chakra	Location	Tapping Point	Affirmation/Chant
Crown Chakra	Top of the Head	Crown of the head	"I am connected to the divine and universal wisdom."
Third Eye Chakra	Between the Eyebrows	Eyebrow/side of the eye	"I trust my intuition and inner wisdom."
Throat Chakra	Throat	Chin/under the nose	"I express my truth clearly and confidently."
Heart Chakra	Center of the Chest	Collarbone	"I am open to love and compassion."
Solar Plexus Chakra	Upper Abdomen	Below the collarbone	"I am confident and in control of my power."

Chakra	Location	Tapping Point	Affirmation/Chant
Sacral Chakra	Lower Abdomen	Below the chest	"I embrace creativity and the flow of life."
Root Chakra	The Base of the Spine	Under the arm	"I am grounded, safe, and secure."

This chart provides an easy-to-follow guide to tapping into your chakra work, with specific affirmations to align each energy center. Use these phrases to deepen your emotional and spiritual healing practice while tapping the corresponding points.

Next, we'll dive into integrating chakra healing with other practices, offering even more tools to enhance your well-being.

Chapter 5:
Integrating Chakra Healing with Other Practices

Picture this: You're on your yoga mat, deep in Tree Pose, when your dog decides it's the *perfect* time to weave between your legs. You wobble, laugh, and somehow manage to find your center again. Moments like this perfectly capture the magic of combining yoga with chakra healing. Yoga and chakra work? They're like peanut butter and jelly—each makes the other a little sweeter, smoother, and more balanced (even when your furry friend has other plans).

Integrating Yoga and Chakra Healing: A Holistic Approach

Yoga isn't just about twisting yourself into pretzel shapes or achieving Instagram-worthy poses. At its core, yoga enhances energy flow throughout your body, promoting balance and well-being. Each yoga pose, or asana, interacts with your chakras, those spinning wheels of energy we've discussed. When you practice yoga mindfully, you're stretching your muscles and aligning your energy centers, making them hum in harmony.

Specific yoga poses target different chakras, helping to clear blockages and enhance energy flow. For instance, grounding poses like Mountain Pose (Tadasana) and Warrior I (Virabhadrasana) are fantastic for the Root Chakra. These poses help you feel steady and grounded, like a tree with deep roots. When your Root Chakra is balanced, you feel secure and connected to the earth.

Heart-opening poses like Camel Pose (Ustrasana) and Cobra Pose (Bhujangasana) work wonders for the Heart Chakra. These poses open your chest, allowing you to give and receive love freely. They help you cultivate compassion and emotional balance, making your heart feel like it's glowing with warmth.

For the Throat Chakra, poses that stimulate the throat area, such as Fish Pose (Matsyasana), are incredibly beneficial. Fish Pose helps open up your throat, improving your communication and self-expression. When your Throat Chakra is balanced, you can speak your truth with clarity and confidence.

Breathwork, or pranayama, is another crucial aspect of yoga and chakra healing. Techniques like Ujjayi breath, where you slightly constrict the back of your throat while breathing, can calm the mind and enhance focus. This breath, often called the "Victorious Breath," creates a soothing sound that helps synchronize your mind and body. Another powerful technique is alternate nostril breathing (Nadi Shodhana). This practice balances energy flow between your brain's left and right hemispheres, promoting a sense of calm and equilibrium. It's like hitting the reset button on your nervous system.

Mindfulness in movement is essential for enhancing chakra awareness during yoga practice. Focus on your breath and body sensations as you move through each pose. This mindfulness helps you tune into your energy centers, making it easier to notice any imbalances. Setting an intention at the beginning of your practice can also enhance your chakra work. Whether you intend to feel more grounded or to open your heart, having a clear focus can guide your practice and deepen its impact.

Imagine starting your practice with a grounding Root Chakra sequence. Begin in Mountain Pose, feeling the earth beneath your feet. Inhale deeply, and as you exhale, root yourself into the ground. Flow into Warrior I, feeling the strength and stability in your legs. This sequence helps you feel connected and secure, setting a solid foundation for your day.

Next, move into a Heart Chakra sequence with Camel and Cobra Pose. Begin on your knees for Camel Pose, placing your hands on your lower back for support. Inhale deeply, and as you exhale, arch your back, lifting your chest toward the sky. Transition into Cobra Pose by lying on your stomach, placing your hands under your shoulders, and lifting your chest as you inhale. These heart-opening poses help release emotional blockages, allowing love and compassion to flow freely.

Finally, focus on the Throat Chakra with Fish Pose. Lie on your back, place your hands under your hips, and lift your chest as you tilt your head back. This pose opens your throat, enhancing your ability to communicate and express yourself. Feel the energy flowing through your Throat Chakra, clearing blockages and promoting clarity.

Incorporating these sequences into your yoga practice can significantly impact your overall well-being. Targeting specific chakras ensures energy flows freely, promoting balance and harmony in your body and mind. Remember, it's not about achieving perfection in each pose but connecting with your energy centers and tuning into your body's needs.

Yoga and chakra healing work hand in hand, offering a holistic approach to well-being. Integrating these practices can profoundly enhance your life, whether you're a seasoned yogi or a beginner. So, roll out your mat, take a deep breath, and let's get those chakras humming in harmony.

Reiki and Chakra Balancing: Energy Work for Healing

Imagine lying comfortably on a massage table, soft music playing in the background, and a gentle warmth spreading through your body. This is what a Reiki session feels like. Reiki, a Japanese form of energy healing, is based on the idea that an unseen "life force energy" flows through us and is what causes us to be alive. Reiki practitioners believe they can channel this energy to promote healing and balance by touching or near the body.

Reiki's roots trace back to the early twentieth century when Mikao Usui, a Japanese Buddhist, developed the practice after a profound spiritual experience. Usui's teachings emphasized the importance of connecting with this universal energy to heal oneself and others. Reiki works by balancing the body's energy, removing blockages, and promoting a free flow of life force. Picture it as a gentle yet powerful way to realign your chakras, helping you feel more centered and at peace.

Specific hand positions target each energy center to balance your chakras with Reiki.

- For the Root Chakra, the practitioner places their hands on the lower back, channeling energy to ground and stabilize you. This can help you feel more secure and connected to the earth.

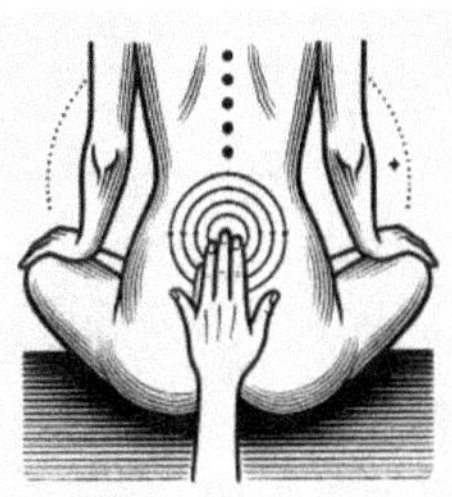

- When working on the Solar Plexus Chakra, hands are placed over the stomach area, encouraging personal power and confidence. Imagine this energy center lighting up, filling you with a sense of self-assuredness and inner strength.

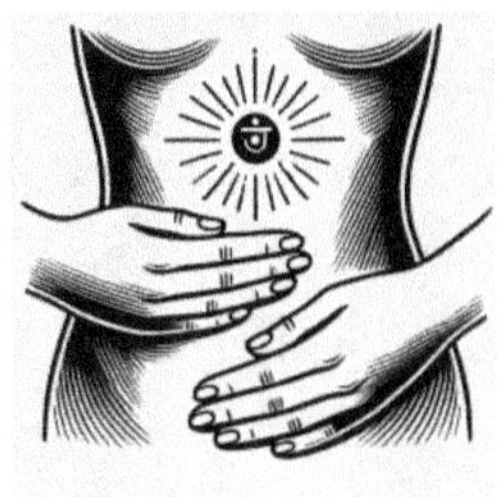

- The Third Eye Chakra, located between your eyebrows, benefits from hands placed gently on the forehead. This position helps enhance intuition and mental clarity. You might feel a sense of insight and understanding as if a fog has lifted from your mind. Each hand position is carefully chosen to align with the specific chakra, ensuring energy flows smoothly and effectively.

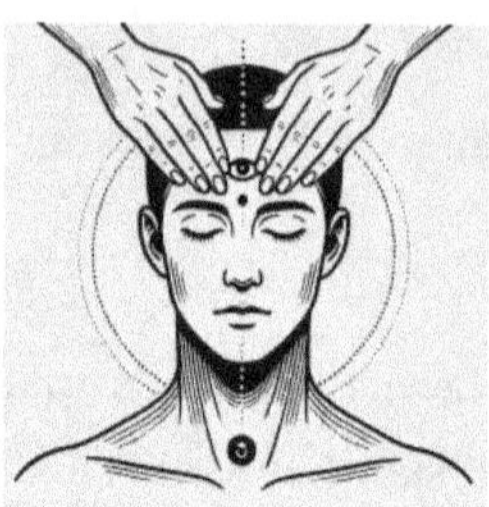

Combining Reiki with chakra healing offers synergistic benefits that can enhance your overall well-being. One of the most immediate effects is enhanced relaxation and stress relief. As the practitioner's hands move over your body, you might feel a wave of calmness washing over you, melting away tension and anxiety. This deep relaxation allows your body to enter a state of healing, where energy flows freely, and blockages are cleared.

Reiki also promotes emotional and spiritual healing. Balancing your chakras can help release stored emotions and traumas, allowing you to process and heal from past wounds. Imagine feeling a sense of emotional release, as if a weight has been lifted from your shoulders. This emotional healing often leads to a deeper connection with your spiritual self, fostering a sense of purpose and inner peace.

Incorporating Reiki into your chakra healing routine is easier than you might think. Start by creating a sacred space for your sessions. Choose a quiet, comfortable area where you won't be disturbed. You might want to set the mood with soft lighting, calming music, and perhaps a few crystals or essential oils. This environment helps you relax and focus on the healing process.

Using crystals and essential oils during Reiki sessions can enhance the experience. For example, placing a piece of Amethyst near your head can amplify the energy flow to your Crown Chakra, promoting spiritual awareness. Similarly, diffusing Lavender essential oil can create a calming atmosphere, helping you relax and open up to the healing energy.

Self-Reiki techniques are also a practical way to maintain balance daily. Start by sitting comfortably and taking a few deep breaths to center yourself. Place your hands on different body parts, focusing on each chakra for a few minutes. You might place your hands on your lower abdomen for the Sacral Chakra or your chest for the Heart Chakra. Visualize energy flowing from your hands into your body, clearing blockages and promoting balance.

Reiki is a powerful tool for balancing your chakras and enhancing your overall well-being. The benefits are profound whether you receive Reiki from a practitioner or practice self-Reiki. You'll find that this gentle, nurturing energy helps you relax, heal, and connect with your inner self.

Tai Chi and Qi Gong: Ancient Practices for Modern Healing

Imagine standing in a serene park, the morning sun warming your face and a gentle breeze rustling the leaves. You begin to move slowly, gracefully mimicking the fluid motions of a dance. This is Tai Chi, an ancient Chinese practice that combines movement, meditation, and breathwork to enhance energy flow and promote well-being. Tai Chi and its sibling, Qi Gong, offer profound benefits for balancing your chakras and improving your overall health.

Tai Chi originated in ancient China as a martial art, but over time, it evolved into a practice focused on health and meditation. Qi Gong, which translates to "energy work," has roots that go back even further. Both practices are built on the philosophy that life force energy or Qi flows through the body along meridian pathways. When Qi flows freely, you experience good health and vitality. When it's blocked, you may feel unwell. Tai Chi and Qi Gong aim to balance this energy, promoting harmony within the body.

Specific movements in Tai Chi and Qi Gong can target different chakras, enhancing their balance and function.

- Grounding movements like "Embrace the Tree" are highly effective for the root chakra. In this stance, you stand with your feet shoulder-width apart, knees slightly bent, and arms curved as if hugging a tree. This pose helps you feel connected to the earth, promoting stability and grounding.

- The Sacral Chakra benefits from flowing movements like "Wave Hands Like Clouds." This graceful motion involves shifting your weight from one foot to the other while gently sweeping your hands across your body. It mimics the ebb and flow of water, enhancing creativity and emotional balance. Imagine your hands moving through the air like waves, each motion bringing a sense of fluidity and ease.

- Expansive movements like "Opening the Heart" are ideal for the Heart Chakra. Stand with your feet together and your arms at your sides. As you inhale, sweep your arms up and out, opening your chest to the sky. This movement fosters love and compassion, inviting positive energy into your heart. Picture your chest expanding with each breath, your heart opening wider to receive and give love.

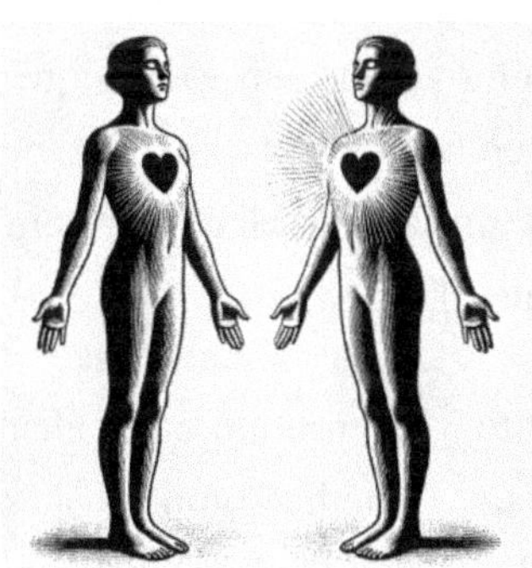

Breath and mindfulness are integral to both Tai Chi and Qi Gong. Coordinating your breath with your movements enhances energy flow and deepens your practice. For instance, in "Embrace the Tree," you might inhale deeply as you bend your knees and exhale as you straighten them. This rhythmic breathing helps you stay present and focused, making each movement more effective.

Maintaining a mindful focus during practice is crucial. As you move, pay attention to the sensations in your body, the rhythm of your breath, and the energy flow. This mindfulness helps you connect with your chakras, making identifying and releasing blockages easier. Set an intention before each session to feel more grounded, open your heart, or enhance your creativity. This intention guides your practice, giving it purpose and direction.

Integrating Tai Chi and Qi Gong with chakra healing offers numerous benefits. Improved energy flow and vitality are among the most immediate. You may notice a surge of energy, a sense of lightness, and increased stamina as you practice. These practices also enhance mental clarity and emotional balance. The slow, deliberate movements calm the mind, reducing stress and anxiety. You may find that you can better handle life's challenges with a clear mind and a steady heart.

Reduced stress and increased relaxation are other significant benefits. Tai Chi and Qi Gong's meditative nature helps lower cortisol levels, the hormone associated with stress. As you move through each sequence, you may feel the tension melting away, replaced by a sense of peace and tranquility. Regular practice can lead to lasting changes, helping you maintain a balanced and harmonious state of being.

Incorporating these ancient practices into your routine can enhance your chakra healing and overall well-being. Whether you're a seasoned practitioner or a complete beginner, Tai Chi and Qi Gong offer accessible and effective ways to balance your energy centers and improve your health. So find a quiet space, take a deep breath, and let the gentle movements guide you toward a more balanced and vibrant life.

Mindfulness and Meditation: Enhancing Chakra Awareness

Picture this: You're sitting in a quiet room, the hum of daily life fading into the background as you focus on nothing but the rhythm of your breath. This is mindfulness, which centers on present-moment awareness and nonjudgment. Mindfulness is about being fully engaged in the here and now, observing your thoughts and sensations without getting caught up in them. It's like giving your mind a much-needed break from its usual overdrive. Meditation, on the other hand, is a practice that takes mindfulness a step further, offering a structured way to focus your mind and dive deeper into your consciousness. There are different types of meditation, such as focused attention, where you concentrate on a single point like your breath or a mantra; open monitoring, where you observe your thoughts without attachment; and loving-kindness, which involves generating feelings of compassion toward yourself and others.

Mindfulness techniques can be incredibly effective for enhancing chakra awareness. One such practice is body scan meditation. In this method, you lie down or sit comfortably and slowly bring your attention to each part of your body, starting from your toes and moving up to your head. As you focus on each area, notice any sensations, tension, or discomfort. This practice helps you tune into your body and identify areas where energy might be blocked. For instance, feeling tightness in your chest could indicate a blockage in your Heart Chakra.

Mindful breathing is another powerful tool. Sit comfortably and close your eyes. Take a deep breath in, and as you exhale, bring your awareness to the sensation of your breath. Notice how it feels as it enters and leaves your nostrils—how your chest and abdomen rise and fall. This simple practice can help you connect with your energy flow, bringing balance to your chakras. Sensory mindfulness, which involves engaging your senses to connect with your chakras, can also be beneficial. For example, you might focus on the taste of a piece of fruit, the sound of birds chirping, or the feeling of a soft blanket against your skin. These practices help ground you and bring your awareness to the present moment.

Meditation practices tailored to each chakra can further enhance your chakra healing. For the Root Chakra, grounding meditation is particularly effective. Sit comfortably and close your eyes. Visualize roots growing from the base of your spine into the earth, anchoring you firmly. Feel the stability and support of the earth beneath you, providing a sense of security and grounding. This practice can help you feel more connected to the earth and reduce anxiety.

For the Heart Chakra, loving-kindness meditation is a beautiful practice. Sit comfortably and close your eyes. Take a few deep breaths to center yourself. Focus on yourself, silently repeating phrases like, "May I be happy. May I be healthy. May I be at peace." Then, gradually extend these wishes to others, starting with someone you love, then to a neutral person, and finally to someone you find challenging. This practice helps cultivate compassion and empathy, opens your heart, and promotes emotional balance.

Silent meditation is particularly beneficial for the Crown Chakra. Find a quiet place, sit comfortably, and close your eyes. Take a few deep breaths to settle your mind. Simply sit in silence, observing your thoughts without attachment. Allow thoughts to come and go, like clouds passing in the sky. This practice helps you connect with your higher self and the universe, fostering a sense of spiritual connection and unity.

The benefits of integrating mindfulness and meditation into your chakra healing practice are profound. One of the most significant benefits is increased self-awareness. Regularly practicing mindfulness and meditation makes you more attuned to your thoughts, emotions, and physical sensations. This heightened awareness allows you to recognize and address any blockages in your chakras before they manifest as physical or emotional issues.

Emotional regulation is another key benefit. Mindfulness and meditation help you develop greater control over your emotions, reducing reactivity and promoting emotional stability. Imagine being able to stay calm and centered even amid a stressful situation. These practices can help you achieve that level of emotional resilience.

Finally, integrating mindfulness and meditation into your chakra healing routine fosters peace and inner harmony. As you connect with your energy centers and bring them into balance, you'll likely experience a deep sense of well-being and contentment. It's like finding your inner sanctuary, a place of calm and tranquility amid the chaos of daily life.

Nutrition and Chakras: Foods That Support Energy Balance

Imagine waking up to the smell of fresh herbs and ripe fruits, your kitchen filled with vibrant colors. It's a feast for your eyes and a boost for your chakras. Nutrition plays a crucial role in supporting chakra health. Different foods influence your energy centers, helping to balance and align them. Think of it as eating the rainbow for your chakras. Each rainbow color corresponds to a different chakra, providing the nutrients and energy needed to support that specific center.

Grounding foods like root vegetables are essential for the root chakra. Carrots, beets, and sweet potatoes, all rich in earthy flavors, provide the stability and grounding that the Root Chakra craves. These root vegetables are nutritious and help you feel more connected to the earth, offering a sense of security. Imagine a hearty stew filled with these root veggies simmering on the stove, filling your home with warmth and comfort.

The Sacral Chakra, which governs creativity and emotions, thrives on orange fruits and vegetables. Rich in beta-carotene, oranges, sweet potatoes, and carrots support this energy center. These foods' vibrant colors and sweet flavors help energize and balance the Sacral Chakra. Picture yourself enjoying a bowl of roasted sweet potatoes with a hint of cinnamon, each bite enhancing your creativity and emotional well-being.

Yellow foods like bananas and corn are fantastic for the Solar Plexus Chakra. This chakra in your upper abdomen is all about personal power and confidence. Bananas can help you feel more empowered with their natural sweetness and energy-boosting properties. Imagine a sunny morning with a smoothie bowl topped with banana slices and a sprinkle of granola, fueling your confidence for the day ahead.

Green leafy vegetables like spinach and kale are essential for the Heart Chakra. These greens are packed with nutrients that promote heart health and emotional balance. Imagine a fresh green smoothie made with spinach, kale, and avocado. Each sip nourishes your heart and fills you with love and compassion. The vibrant green color and refreshing taste can help open your Heart Chakra, allowing love to flow freely.

Blueberries and blackberries are perfect for the Throat Chakra. Their deep blue hues resonate with the Throat Chakra, enhancing communication and self-expression. Picture a bowl of fresh blueberries, each bite helping to clear blockages and improve your ability to speak your truth. Imagine adding them to your morning yogurt or oatmeal, starting your day with a boost for your Throat Chakra.

Purple foods, like grapes and eggplant, benefit the Third Eye Chakra, located between your eyebrows. These foods support intuition and insight, helping you connect with your inner wisdom. Imagine a salad with slices of purple cabbage and grapes, each bite nourishing your Third Eye Chakra and enhancing your intuitive abilities.

Light-colored foods like garlic and onions are ideal for the Crown Chakra. They help to clear and balance the Crown Chakra, promoting spiritual connection and enlightenment. Picture a simple dish of roasted garlic and onions, their flavors melding together to create a delicious meal that supports your spiritual well-being.

Incorporating these chakra-supportive foods into your diet can be both delicious and beneficial. For instance, a Root Chakra stew made with carrots, beets, and sweet potatoes can provide grounding and nourishment. Imagine simmering these root vegetables with herbs and spices, creating a hearty, comforting stew that fills you with warmth and stability. Or consider a Heart Chakra smoothie made with spinach, kale, and avocado. Blend these greens with a splash of almond milk and a drizzle of honey, creating a refreshing and nutritious smoothie that supports your heart health and emotional balance.

Mindful eating practices can further enhance the benefits of these chakra-supportive foods. Eating with intention and gratitude can transform your meals into meditation. Before each meal, express gratitude for the food and its nourishing properties. Savor each bite, paying attention to the flavors, textures, and aromas. This mindful approach to eating helps you connect with your food and your body, promoting balance and harmony in your energy centers.

Incorporating these foods and mindful eating practices into your daily routine can support your chakra health and overall well-being. Imagine each meal as an opportunity to nourish not just your body but your energy centers, creating a balanced and harmonious life.

Creating a Balanced Lifestyle: Daily Practices for Chakra Health

Living a balanced lifestyle is crucial for maintaining healthy chakras and overall well-being. Your physical, emotional, and spiritual health are deeply interconnected, like threads in a tapestry. When one aspect is out of balance, it can affect the others, creating a ripple effect throughout your life. Daily habits play a significant role in influencing your energy flow and chakra balance. Simple practices can make a huge difference in how you feel and function.

Starting your day with grounding rituals can set a positive tone. Stretching when you first wake up helps to awaken your body and mind, preparing you for the day ahead. Pair this with a few deep breaths, inhaling through your nose and exhaling through your mouth, to help center your energy. Adding affirmations can further enhance this practice. Statements like "I am grounded and secure" or "I am open to new opportunities" can help align your chakras and set a positive mindset for the day.

Midday energy boosts are equally important. Life gets busy, and getting caught up in the hustle and bustle is easy. Taking a quick break for a short meditation or a few yoga poses can re-energize you and keep your chakras balanced. Even five minutes of mindful breathing or a gentle stretch can make a big difference. Find a quiet corner or step outside if you can. Focus on your breath, letting go of any tension or stress. These small breaks help maintain energy flow and keep you balanced and centered.

As the day winds down, evening relaxation techniques can help you release the day's stress and prepare for restful sleep. Journaling is a great way to reflect on your day and process lingering emotions. Write about what went well, what challenged you, and what you're grateful for. This practice can help clear your mind and balance your chakras before bed. Aromatherapy can also be incredibly soothing. Diffuse calming essential oils like lavender or chamomile to create a peaceful atmosphere. Add gentle stretches to your routine, focusing on releasing tension from your body. These practices help you unwind and ensure a balanced end to your day.

Balancing productivity with rest is crucial for maintaining chakra health. Getting caught up in the never-ending to-do list is easy, but not setting boundaries can lead to burnout and energy imbalances. Make it a priority to set clear boundaries for work and personal time. When you're working, focus entirely on your tasks. When it's time to rest, allow yourself to fully relax without guilt. Prioritizing self-care and downtime is essential. Whether reading a book, taking a bath, or simply sitting silently, make time for activities that recharge your energy. This balance helps keep your chakras aligned and your energy flowing smoothly.

Spending time in nature is like hitting the reset button for your chakras. It grounds you, connects you to the Earth, and balances your energy. And here's a fun fact—did you know that walking barefoot on the earth, feeling the grass or sand under your feet, can help recharge your Root Chakra? Yep, your feet have energy receptors, and when you let them make direct contact with the ground, you're syncing up with the Earth's natural energy. Don't let your rubber soles interfere with your grounding—kick off those shoes and let the Earth do its magic.

Next time you're out for a walk in the park or on the beach, take a moment to *feel* the earth beneath your feet. Breathe deeply and notice how it instantly makes you feel more grounded, centered, and secure. It's like nature is giving you a big, supportive hug.

And while you're at it, let's get your Sacral Chakra dancing! Put on your favorite song and let your body move. Dancing isn't just fun—it's a brilliant way to release stuck emotions and get that creative energy flowing. Your Sacral Chakra will be buzzing with joy.

Want to supercharge the experience? Try practicing yoga outdoors. Something about the fresh air and the sounds of nature takes your practice to the next level. Each breath helps align your energy, promoting balance and harmony across all your chakras. It's like Mother Nature's gift to your soul.

Incorporating these daily practices into your routine can significantly impact your overall well-being. Focusing on small, consistent habits can help you maintain balanced chakras and a healthy energy flow. Remember, it's not about perfection but finding what works for you and making it a part of your daily life. The more you tune into your body and energy centers, the easier it becomes to maintain balance and harmony.

As you continue exploring the world of chakra healing, remember that it's a journey of self-discovery and growth. Each practice, whether grounding rituals, midday energy boosts, or evening relaxation techniques, brings you closer to a balanced and harmonious life. Embrace these practices with an open heart and mind, knowing that every small step you take contributes to your overall well-being and spiritual growth.

Fun Facts

Now that we've explored how yoga, nature, and energy work all contribute to balancing and healing your chakras, let's add some more depth and fun to your practice. These surprising and fascinating facts will help you see how your everyday actions and nature's gifts constantly support your chakra health in ways you might not have known. Prepare for a few "aha" moments as we dive into these fantastic insights!

Your Chakras Love the Sun: Spending time in natural sunlight isn't just great for your mood—it helps balance your Solar Plexus Chakra, too! Sunlight is connected to this energy center, which governs personal power and confidence. Daily sunshine can empower you in ways you might not even realize. So go ahead and soak up that solar energy!

Tree Pose, Root Power: Ever notice how steady and grounded you feel in Tree Pose (Vrksasana)? This classic yoga pose is a Root Chakra booster. Fun fact: The subtle act of balancing in this pose strengthens the connection between your body and the Earth's energy. With each breath, you're not just balancing physically but also tapping into a deeper sense of stability and security.

Crystals and Chakra Alignment: Did you know that certain crystals resonate with specific chakras? For example, Amethyst works wonders for your Crown Chakra, helping you access higher states of consciousness and spiritual awareness. Meanwhile, Rose Quartz is known for its Heart Chakra healing, which promotes love and emotional balance. Carrying or meditating with these stones can help align your energy with their natural vibrations.

Sound Healing for Your Chakras: Here's a fun fact: Each of your chakras is associated with a specific sound frequency or "vibration." Sound healing practices, like singing bowls or tuning forks, are tuned to these specific frequencies. For example, the note "C" corresponds to the Root Chakra, and "G" resonates with the Throat Chakra. Sound healing can clear blockages and align your chakras, turning your body into a symphony of harmony!

Pranayama = Brain Sync: Did you know that alternate nostril breathing (Nadi Shodhana) helps synchronize your brain's left and right hemispheres? It's like giving your mind a tune-up! Balancing prana (life force) flow through both nostrils, this simple breathwork technique aligns your Third Eye Chakra, promoting clarity, focus, and intuitive insight. It's like hitting the reset button for your entire nervous system.

Vagal Tone and Chakra Balance: Cultivating Harmony

Let's talk about the vagus nerve—the unsung hero of your body's "rest and recharge" system. This extraordinary nerve, often called the "wandering nerve," is like the body's ultimate communicator, running from your brainstem through your heart, lungs, and gut. It's responsible for all those essential, calming functions like slowing your heart rate, aiding digestion, and boosting your immune system. But here's where it gets really cool: The vagus nerve isn't just about keeping your body in check—it's also a key player in balancing your chakras and connecting your physical health with your emotional and spiritual well-being.

Picture this: When you take a deep breath, not only are you calming your mind, but you're also stimulating your vagus nerve, which can directly influence your energy flow. It's like giving your nervous system and your chakras a double high-five! For instance, deep breathing relaxes your body and opens up your Third Eye Chakra, helping clear mental fog and spark intuition. When you practice yoga poses that open the heart, you engage your Heart Chakra and the vagus nerve, which helps balance emotions and foster compassion.

Oh, and don't forget about vagal tone. A strong vagal tone means your vagus nerve is in top shape, which means better emotional resilience and easier chakra alignment. Practices like diaphragmatic breathing, meditation, and even chanting "OM" (yep, that sound stimulates the vagus nerve, too!) can boost your vagal tone and clear energy blockages. It's like having a built-in reset button for your body and soul, all while keeping your chakras buzzing in harmony.

So, the next time you're working on balancing your chakras, remember your vagus nerve is right there with you, bridging the gap between your physical health and spiritual growth. Stimulating this nerve, whether through deep breathing, cold exposure, or your daily yoga practice, is key to aligning your body, mind, and spirit.

Now that you know how the vagus nerve is the ultimate bridge between physical health and chakra balance, let's dive into a few more awesome details that will deepen your understanding of this powerful connection.

1. Gut-Brain Connection & the Solar Plexus Chakra

- The vagus nerve is deeply connected to the gut, sometimes called the "second brain." This connection ties directly to the Solar Plexus Chakra, which is responsible for personal power, self-confidence, and digestion. Improving vagal tone can help balance this chakra, boosting your physical digestion and how you "digest" emotions like stress and self-doubt.

- **Pro Tip:** Improve gut health through nutrition (probiotics, fiber-rich foods), enhance vagal tone, and support a balanced Solar Plexus Chakra.

2. Cold Exposure for Vagus Stimulation

- Did you know cold showers or splashing cold water on your face activate the vagus nerve? This simple, effective practice sends signals to the brain to calm the nervous system and enhance emotional regulation. Since the vagus nerve runs through the neck, it can also stimulate the throat chakra, promoting clear communication and truthfulness.
- **Fun Detail:** Mention that Wim Hof, the "Iceman," uses cold exposure and breathing techniques to enhance vagal tone, which aligns both body and energy systems.

3. Vagus Nerve & Heart Rate Variability (HRV)

- Heart rate variability indicates vagal tone and is linked to the Heart Chakra. The more resilient your vagus nerve (high HRV), the more balanced your Heart Chakra will likely be. This means you're emotionally balanced and more capable of gracefully handling life's stresses.
- **Quick Fact:** Athletes often measure HRV to track recovery and performance. Breathwork or meditation can improve HRV and enhance Heart Chakra energy.

4. Singing & Humming for Throat Chakra & Vagus Stimulation

- Because the vagus nerve passes through the vocal cords, vocal exercises like singing, chanting, and humming stimulate it. This also directly supports the Throat Chakra. So, next time you belt out your favorite song in the shower, remember you're not just boosting your mood—you're also tuning your chakras and vagus nerve!

5. Vagus Nerve as the Gateway to the Parasympathetic Nervous System

- The vagus nerve is the key to unlocking the parasympathetic nervous system—our body's "rest and digest" mode. It directly opposes the "fight or flight" response triggered by stress, meaning vagus nerve stimulation can help unblock energy in the Sacral Chakra (often tied to emotional trauma) and the Root Chakra (linked to safety and survival).
- Illustration showing the vagus nerve and its path through the body, from the brainstem down the neck, and connecting to major organs like the heart, lungs, and digestive system.

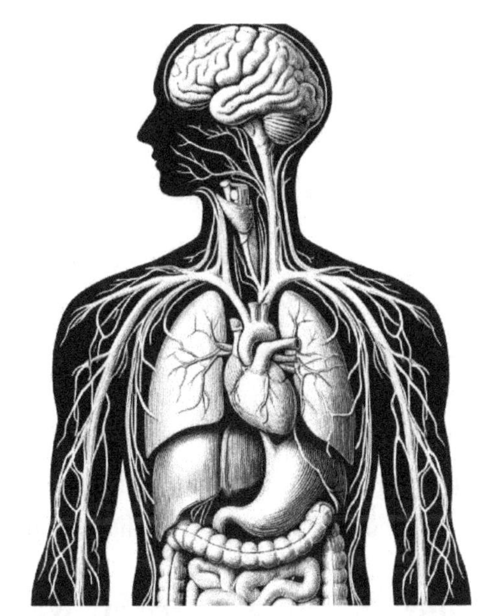

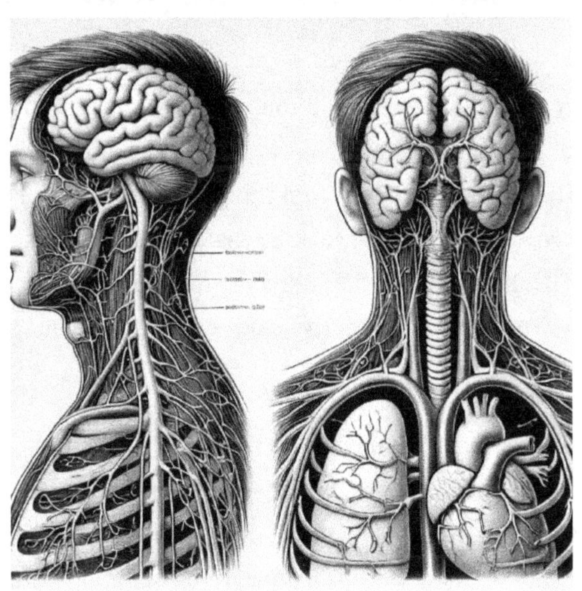

Chapter 6:
Practical Applications and Daily Practices

Imagine waking up groggy and barely coherent, and you first reach for your phone. You scroll through emails and social media, and before you know it, you've wasted thirty minutes and feel even more drained. Sound familiar? Now, imagine beginning your day differently. Picture yourself stepping out of bed, feeling grounded, centered, and ready to face whatever comes your way. This chapter is about creating a morning routine that sets a positive tone for your day by balancing your chakras right from the start.

Morning Routines: Starting Your Day with Balanced Chakras

How you start your day can set the tone for everything. When you begin with balanced chakras, you're laying a solid foundation for your overall well-being. Aligning your energy first thing in the morning helps you feel grounded, focused, and ready to tackle whatever comes your way. This is not just about feeling good at the moment; it has lasting benefits that can influence your mood, productivity, and even how you handle stress throughout the day.

Grounding exercises are a fantastic way to kick off your morning. Try standing barefoot on the earth for the Root Chakra, which is all about stability and security. If you have a backyard or a nearby park, this is a great way to feel instantly connected to nature. Even standing barefoot on your living room floor can work if that's not an option. Visualize roots growing from your feet into the ground. Picture these roots anchoring you firmly, providing stability and security. This simple exercise can make you feel more grounded and present, setting a solid foundation for the rest of your day.

Affirmations are another powerful tool to start your day on a positive note. For the Root Chakra, try saying, *"I am safe, secure, and grounded."* This affirmation reinforces the sense of stability and security you've cultivated through your grounding exercise. For the Solar Plexus Chakra, which deals with personal power and confidence, an affirmation like *"I am confident and powerful"* can set a positive tone for your day. These affirmations are like planting seeds of positivity in your mind, which can grow and flourish throughout the day.

Incorporating a quick yoga sequence into your morning routine can also work wonders for balancing your chakras. One of the best sequences for this is the Sun Salutation. This series of poses energizes the body and targets multiple chakras, making it an efficient way to align your energy centers. Start with Mountain Pose, standing tall and feeling grounded. Move into a forward bend to release tension in the lower back and hamstrings, then transition into a plank to engage your core and Solar Plexus Chakra. Flow through to an upward dog to open your Heart Chakra, and finish with a downward dog to stretch and balance your entire body.

The beauty of a morning routine focusing on chakra alignment is that it doesn't have to be time-consuming. Even dedicating 10–15 minutes can significantly affect how you feel throughout the day. The key is consistency. Make these practices a regular part of your morning, and you'll notice the benefits accumulating over time. You'll feel more grounded, focused, and ready to face the day's challenges with a balanced and positive mindset.

Consider setting up a dedicated space for your morning routine to make it easier. This could be a corner of your bedroom or living room, equipped with a yoga mat, a few crystals, and a small diffuser with essential oils. Having a designated space can make it easier to stick to your routine and create a sense of ritual. Plus, it gives you something to look forward to each morning—a peaceful, sacred space to start your day feeling balanced and centered.

Incorporating these practices into your morning routine can transform how you start your day and experience the entire day. You'll find you're more resilient, focused, and in tune with your needs and energy levels. And that, my friend, is a powerful way to live.

Evening Practices: Winding Down with Chakra Healing

Evening rituals are your secret weapon for winding down and preparing for a restful night's sleep. Think of them as a way to gently release the stress and tension accumulated throughout the day, allowing you to transition into a state of relaxation and healing. When you take time to engage in evening practices, you're not just setting yourself up for a good night's sleep; you're promoting emotional and physical healing. This can help you wake up feeling refreshed and balanced, ready to face a new day with a clear mind and open heart.

One effective way to wind down is through a relaxing meditation practice. For the Heart Chakra, try a loving-kindness meditation. Find a quiet space, sit comfortably, and close your eyes. Take a few deep breaths to center yourself. Then, focus on the center of your chest, where the Heart Chakra is located. Imagine a warm, green light glowing from this area. As you inhale, let this light expand, filling your chest with warmth and compassion. As you exhale, imagine sending this loving energy out into the world. Think of someone you love, and silently repeat phrases like, *"May you be happy, may you be healthy, may you be at peace."* This practice fosters self-compassion and emotional balance, making letting go of the day's stress easier.

A guided visualization can help you connect with a higher consciousness for the Crown Chakra. Lie down in a comfortable position and close your eyes. Visualize a soft, violet light at the top of your head. As you breathe in, imagine this light growing brighter and more intense. Picture it opening up like a lotus flower, connecting you to the universe. Feel the sense of peace and spiritual connection this brings. This visualization calms the mind and helps you feel more connected to something greater than yourself, promoting overall well-being.

Journaling is another powerful tool for reflecting on your day and releasing lingering emotions. For the Sacral Chakra, which governs creativity and emotions, write about your creative expressions and feelings for a few minutes. What did you create today? How did it make you feel? This practice helps you process your emotions and celebrate your creative achievements, fostering a sense of fulfillment. For the Throat Chakra, which is all about communication, reflect on how you expressed yourself throughout the day. Were there moments when you felt unheard or struggled to articulate your thoughts? Writing about these experiences can help you identify any blockages and find ways to improve your self-expression.

Creating a peaceful environment is crucial for winding down. Soft lighting can make a big difference. Consider using lamps with warm, dimmable bulbs or even a few candles to create a calming atmosphere. Calming scents can also set the mood. Essential oils like Lavender or Chamomile are perfect for relaxation. You can diffuse them in your bedroom or apply drops to your pillow. Arranging crystals and calming objects in your space can further enhance the environment. Crystals like Amethyst and Rose Quartz have soothing energies that promote peace and emotional healing. Place them on your nightstand or under your pillow to benefit from their calming properties.

Incorporating these evening practices into your routine can significantly improve your physical and emotional well-being. By taking time to unwind and release the day's stress, you create a foundation for better sleep and overall well-being. These practices are an excellent way to connect with yourself, fostering a deeper self-awareness and balance. So, take a moment each evening to engage in these rituals. Your mind, body, and spirit will thank you.

Quick Chakra Balancing Techniques: On-the-Go Solutions

We live in a fast-paced world where finding time for self-care can feel like a luxury. That's why quick chakra balancing techniques are so invaluable. They offer easy-to-implement practices that can fit into even the busiest schedules. Imagine you're rushing to a meeting, feeling frazzled and off-balance. Or perhaps you're standing in line at the grocery store, overwhelmed by the day's demands. These are the moments when quick chakra balancing can be a game-changer. These techniques help you regain your center, manage stress, and keep your energy flowing smoothly, all without needing a dedicated block of time.

Breathwork is one of the simplest yet most effective ways to balance your chakras on the go. Deep belly breathing can help you regain control and confidence for the Solar Plexus Chakra. Sit or stand comfortably, place your hand on your abdomen, and take a deep breath through your nose, allowing your belly to expand. Hold for a moment, then exhale slowly through your mouth, feeling your belly contract. Repeat this a few times to feel more centered and in control. For the Third Eye Chakra, alternate nostril breathing can enhance mental clarity. Close your right nostril with your thumb, inhale deeply through your left nostril, then close your left nostril with your ring finger and exhale through your right nostril. Continue this pattern for a few cycles to clear your mind and sharpen your focus.

Mini-meditations are perfect for those moments when you need a quick reset. If you feel ungrounded while standing in line, try a grounding visualization for your Root Chakra. Close your eyes (if you can) and imagine roots growing from the soles of your feet deep into the earth. Feel the stability and support of the ground beneath you, anchoring you firmly. This simple visualization can help you feel more stable and present. For a quick Heart Chakra boost, take a brief loving-kindness meditation break. Close your eyes and take a deep breath. Focus on the center of your chest and imagine a warm, green light glowing there. Silently repeat phrases like, "May I be happy, may I be healthy, may I be at peace." This can be done in a minute or two, leaving you feeling more compassionate and connected.

Essential oils are another fantastic tool for quick chakra balancing. Try inhaling Orange essential oil to boost creativity and balance your Sacral Chakra. Carry a small bottle with you and take a deep whiff whenever you need a burst of inspiration or emotional uplift. The bright, citrusy aroma can invigorate your senses and enhance your creative energy. For the Throat Chakra, apply Peppermint oil to the throat area. The incredible, refreshing scent can clear your mind and improve communication, making it easier to express yourself clearly. Keep a small roller bottle in your bag for easy daily access.

These quick techniques are not just convenient; they're highly effective in keeping your energy balanced and your mind focused. Whether using breathwork to regain control, mini-meditations to center yourself, or essential oils for a quick boost, these practices can seamlessly fit into your daily routine. They offer immediate benefits, helping you navigate even the most hectic days with calm and balance. The key is to make these techniques a regular part of your toolkit so you can easily pull them out whenever you need a quick reset.

Incorporating these quick chakra balancing techniques into your daily life can significantly affect how you feel and function. They offer practical, accessible ways to maintain your energy and well-being, no matter how busy your schedule gets. So, next time you find yourself feeling off-balance, remember these simple yet powerful tools. They can help you stay grounded, focused, and ready to face whatever comes your way.

Chakra Healing for Stress Relief: Techniques and Tips

Understanding the connection between stress and chakra imbalances is key to effective stress management. When stressed, your body reacts in ways that can throw your chakras out of balance. For instance, stress can make you feel ungrounded, impacting your Root Chakra. You might experience anxiety, fear, or even physical symptoms like lower back pain. The Solar Plexus Chakra, responsible for personal power and confidence, can also take a hit, leading to feelings of helplessness or low self-esteem. Over time, these imbalances can manifest as chronic stress, affecting overall well-being.

One of the first signs of stress-related chakra blockages is physical discomfort. You might feel tightness in your chest, indicating an imbalance in the Heart Chakra. Or you might struggle with digestive issues, a sign that your Solar Plexus Chakra is out of whack. Emotionally, stress can make you feel overwhelmed, anxious, or irritable. These are all red flags that your energy centers need some attention. Recognizing these signs early on can help you take proactive steps to restore balance and alleviate stress.

Breathing exercises are a simple yet powerful way to relieve stress and balance your chakras. For the Root Chakra, deep diaphragmatic breathing can work wonders. Sit comfortably and place one hand on your chest and the other on your abdomen. Inhale deeply through your nose, allowing your abdomen to expand. Hold your breath for a moment, then exhale slowly through your mouth. This breathing helps ground you, making you feel more secure and stable. For the Crown Chakra, try slow, rhythmic breathing. Sit in a quiet space, close your eyes, and breathe slowly through your nose. Hold for a few seconds, then exhale slowly through your mouth. This calms the mind and promotes a sense of peace and relaxation.

Certain yoga poses are also excellent for stress relief. Child's Pose is a go-to for overall relaxation. Kneel on the floor, sit back on your heels, and then fold forward, extending your arms in front of you. Rest your forehead on the mat and breathe deeply. This pose soothes the nervous system and helps release tension. Legs-Up-the-Wall Pose is another great option. Lie on your back and extend your legs up a wall. This pose calms the nervous system, reduces stress, and promotes relaxation. It's like a mini-vacation for your body and mind.

Creating a stress-relief toolkit can give you easy access to calming resources whenever needed. Start by including crystals like Amethyst, known for its calming energy. Keep a small piece in your pocket or place it on your nightstand. Preparing calming herbal teas like Chamomile and Lavender can also be incredibly soothing. Brew a cup in the evening or whenever you feel stressed. Making tea can be a calming ritual, providing a moment of mindfulness in a busy day.

Your stress-relief toolkit can include a journal for jotting down thoughts and feelings, a small bottle of lavender essential oil for quick aromatherapy, and perhaps a guided meditation app on your phone. Having these readily available tools can make managing stress easier as it arises, helping you stay balanced and calm even in challenging situations. The key is finding what works best for you and making these tools routine.

Incorporating these techniques and tools into your daily life can significantly affect how you manage stress. Understanding the connection between stress and chakra imbalances allows you to take proactive steps to maintain your energy flow and overall well-being. Whether it's through breathing exercises, yoga poses, or a personalized stress-relief toolkit, these practices provide practical, accessible ways to keep stress in check and your chakras balanced.

Using Technology: Apps and Tools for Chakra Healing

Technology can be a powerful ally in your chakra healing practice in this digital age. Imagine having a personal guide in your pocket to help you balance your energy centers anytime, anywhere. That's the beauty of using apps and tools for chakra healing—they offer accessibility and convenience, making incorporating these practices into your daily life easier. Whether you're a tech enthusiast or a newbie, you'll find that these digital resources can significantly enhance your chakra work.

Apps designed for chakra healing can offer a range of features, from guided meditations to yoga sequences, all tailored to balance specific chakras. For instance, meditation apps like Headspace provide guided sessions focusing on chakra healing aspects. You can choose a meditation for your Root Chakra to feel more grounded or one for your Heart Chakra to foster love and compassion. These guided sessions take the guesswork out of your practice, offering clear instructions and soothing voices to guide you through each step.

Yoga apps like Glo offer sequences specifically designed to target different chakras. Imagine rolling out your yoga mat, opening the app, and finding a sequence focusing on your Solar Plexus Chakra, boosting your confidence and personal power. Whether you're a seasoned yogi or a beginner, these apps provide a variety of classes that can fit your skill level and schedule. It's like having a personal yoga instructor available at your convenience, making staying consistent with your practice easier.

Sound therapy apps are another fantastic resource. Apps like Insight Timer offer a wide range of soundscapes, from Tibetan singing bowls to binaural beats, each designed to resonate with different chakras. You can listen to a specific frequency to balance your Third Eye Chakra while you work or play a soothing soundscape to help you unwind and balance your Crown Chakra before bed. These sound therapy sessions can quickly and effectively align your energy, even during a busy day.

Online resources and communities are also invaluable. Websites with articles and tutorials on chakra healing can give you a deeper understanding of your practice. You can find step-by-step guides, expert advice, and even scientific studies supporting chakra work's benefits. Online forums and social media groups offer a sense of community, where you can share your experiences, ask questions, and learn from others on a similar path. These communities can be a source of inspiration and support, making your chakra healing practice feel less solitary and more connected.

Wearable technology is another exciting frontier in chakra healing. Bright jewelry, like chakra bracelets with sensors, can track your energy levels and provide real-time feedback. Imagine a bracelet that vibrates when your energy is low, reminding you to take a moment to breathe and balance your chakras. Apps that sync with wearable devices can offer insights into your energy patterns, helping you understand how different activities and environments affect your chakras. This data can be incredibly useful for fine-tuning your practice and making informed decisions about your well-being.

The potential of technology in chakra healing is vast. These digital tools make it easier to stay consistent, offering reminders, tracking progress, and providing guided practices that can fit seamlessly into your daily routine. They offer accessibility that can be particularly beneficial for those who may not have easy access to in-person classes or workshops. With the right apps and tools, you can make chakra healing a regular part of your life, enhancing your well-being with the help of technology.

So, whether you're using an app for guided meditation, a wearable device to track your energy, or an online community for support, technology can offer valuable resources to enhance your chakra healing practice. These tools make it easier to stay consistent, track your progress, and access expert guidance from your home.

Overcoming Plateaus in Your Healing Journey

Have you ever felt stuck in a rut, no matter how many times you meditate or practice yoga? That's what we call a healing plateau. It's like hitting a wall in your chakra healing practice, where progress stalls. But don't worry; this is a natural part of the healing process. Think of it as your body's way of signaling that deeper issues need your attention. Maybe there's an emotional wound you haven't fully addressed or a physical habit blocking your energy flow. Recognizing these plateaus is the first step to overcoming them.

So, how do you break through these plateaus? One effective strategy is to try new meditation or yoga practices. If you've been doing the same routine for months, your body and mind might need a fresh approach. Experiment with meditation techniques, like guided visualizations or mantra meditations, to see which resonates with you. Similarly, explore new yoga poses or sequences that target different chakras. This can reignite your passion for your practice and help you overcome stagnation.

Another powerful tool is seeking guidance from a mentor or practitioner. Sometimes, an outside perspective can provide insights you have missed. Find a trusted healer or yoga instructor specializing in chakras and schedule a few sessions. They can offer personalized advice and techniques tailored to your unique needs. It's like having a coach to help you navigate the tricky parts of your healing journey. Their expertise can provide the push you need to get back on track.

Engaging in self-reflection and journaling can also be incredibly beneficial. Take time to write about your experiences, focusing on any areas where you feel stuck. Ask yourself questions like, "What emotions am I avoiding?" or "What patterns keep recurring in my life?" This can help uncover underlying issues that might be contributing to your plateau. Reflecting on your journey so far can also remind you of how far you've come, providing motivation to keep going.

Staying motivated during challenging periods can be tricky, but setting new, inspiring goals can help. Break down your healing journey into smaller, achievable milestones. Celebrate each victory, no matter how small. This can provide a sense of accomplishment and keep you motivated to continue.

Joining a supportive community or group can also make a world of difference. Surround yourself with like-minded individuals who are on a similar path. Share your experiences, challenges, and successes. Their support and encouragement can lift you when you're feeling down.

A few years ago, I hit a meditation plateau. Do you know that feeling when you're putting in the time, sitting there with all the right intentions, but something just feels stuck? That was me. No matter how much I meditated, I felt like I wasn't getting anywhere.

So, I did what any slightly frustrated, spiritually-seeking person would do— I sought help. I reached out to a seasoned meditation teacher who introduced me to new techniques completely different from what I was used to. Let me tell you, at first, I thought, "This is *way* out of my comfort zone." But I decided to give it a shot, and within just a few weeks, I felt an undeniable shift in my energy, mindset, and overall practice. It was like my meditation practice got a fresh pair of wings!

Now, I'm sharing these same techniques with you. Whether you've been practicing meditation for years or just getting started, these methods will help you break through those mental blocks and reach new levels of clarity, relaxation, and growth.

- **Heightened Mental Clarity:** After incorporating the new technique, you might have noticed your thoughts becoming clearer, with less mental chatter. Your focus improved, making it easier to remain present during meditation.

- **Deeper Emotional Awareness:** You may have experienced a shift in how you processed emotions—feeling more in tune with underlying emotions or triggers, which allowed you to release pent-up stress or anxiety.

- **Increased Physical Relaxation:** The new technique helped you achieve a more profound sense of relaxation in your body, noticing a drop in tension in areas like the shoulders, neck, or back.

- **Enhanced Energy Flow:** You could describe how your energy felt more balanced, perhaps with fewer blockages and a renewed sense of vitality. This may have translated into feeling more grounded, calm, and centered throughout your day.

- **Shift in Mindset or Perspective:** With the fresh technique, you may have seen a change in your approach to challenges, becoming more open to new perspectives and releasing limiting beliefs. Your attitude toward meditation and life may have become more positive and expansive.

Another example is a friend who found renewed energy by trying new practices. She had been practicing yoga for years but felt like her progress had stalled. She explored Tai Chi, an ancient Chinese practice combining movement, meditation, and breathwork. The slow, deliberate movements of Tai Chi helped her connect with her energy in a new way. Not only did it help her break through her plateau, but it also added a new dimension to her overall wellness routine.

Now, before we move forward, let's take a moment to reflect. Self-reflection is essential to growth, especially when working with your chakras. These questions are designed to help you check in with yourself and your progress. Take your time with them—there are no right or wrong answers, only insights waiting to be discovered.

Self-Reflection Questions

1. **Morning Routine:** How does your current morning routine make you feel? What changes can you incorporate grounding, breathing, or affirmations into your day to start with more balance?

2. **Evening Reflection:** When was the last time you intentionally wound down at night with chakra healing in mind? Which chakra needs the most attention in your evening routine, and how will you focus on it?

3. **Quick Fixes:** Think about a recent stressful moment—did you use quick chakra balancing techniques like breathwork or essential oils? How did it change your feelings, and which method will you keep in your toolkit?

4. **Plateau Breakthrough:** Have you ever experienced a plateau in your meditation or wellness practice? What new technique could you try to shake things up and reignite your progress?

5. **Creative Space:** Do you have a dedicated space for your daily practices? If not, how can you create a small, sacred area in your home to anchor your energy and boost consistency?

As we dive deeper into chakra healing practices and daily routines, it's important to remember that this journey is both a mental and emotional process. Sometimes, a simple quote can spark inspiration and help us see things from a new perspective. Here are two powerful thoughts to remember as you explore your path to balance and wellness.

"Balance begins the moment you breathe with intention. When you center your   energy, you become the master of your mind, body, and soul."

"Healing doesn't happen overnight. It's in the small, daily practices where the magic of transformation truly takes place."

In the next chapter, we'll explore advanced techniques and continuous learning, diving deeper into the intricacies of chakra healing and expanding your practice to new heights.

Chapter 7:
Case Studies and Personal Stories

Have you ever been stuck in traffic, feeling the world's weight pressing down on your shoulders, and wondered, "How did I get here?" Life can be overwhelming; sometimes, it feels like you're carrying an invisible backpack filled with stress, heartbreak, and spiritual disconnection. It's easy to feel alone in moments like these, but you're not. Real-life stories of transformation can serve as powerful reminders that change is possible. They connect us on a deeper emotional level and illustrate the abstract concepts of chakra healing in a way that resonates with our experiences.

Take Sarah, for example. When I first met her, she was a bundle of nerves, juggling a high-pressure job and the demands of daily life. Her anxiety was through the roof, and she felt like she was constantly racing against the clock. Sarah's stress levels were wreaking havoc on her well-being. She couldn't sleep, and her mind was always in overdrive. One day, she decided enough was enough and turned to chakra healing out of sheer desperation. She started with daily meditation focused on her Root Chakra, using grounding techniques to stabilize her energy. She also incorporated yoga into her routine, practicing poses that targeted her Solar Plexus and Heart Chakras to build confidence and emotional resilience. Over time, Sarah noticed a significant shift. She felt calmer, more centered, and better equipped to handle stress. Her anxiety lessened, and she began to sleep better. Today, Sarah is a living testament to the power of chakra balancing, enjoying a newfound sense of serenity and control over her life.

Then there's Alex. Heartbreak had left him feeling shattered and emotionally numb. He struggled to move on, and his Heart Chakra desperately needed healing. Alex's journey began with forgiveness exercises. Each night, he wrote letters of forgiveness—not to send but to release his emotional baggage. He also practiced heart-opening yoga poses like Camel Pose and

Bridge Pose to physically and emotionally open his chest. Slowly but surely, Alex started to feel a shift. The walls around his heart began to crumble, allowing love and compassion to flow in. His emotional health improved, and he formed more profound, meaningful connections. Alex's transformation didn't happen overnight, but through persistent chakra work, he emerged from his heartbreak stronger and more open to love than ever before.

Maria's story is another powerful example. She felt spiritually disconnected, like a ship adrift without a compass. Her life lacked a sense of purpose, and she yearned for a deeper connection to something greater than herself. Maria focused on her Crown Chakra, the gateway to higher consciousness and spiritual enlightenment. She began a daily practice of Crown Chakra meditation, visualizing a violet light entering the top of her head and filling her with a sense of peace and connection. Maria also immersed herself in spiritual texts, finding solace and wisdom in their teachings. As she deepened her practice, Maria experienced profound shifts. She felt a renewed sense of purpose and inner peace, as if she had finally found her true north. Her spiritual reconnection transformed her life, filling it with meaning and fulfillment.

These stories highlight the transformative power of chakra healing. They show us that no matter how overwhelming life may seem, there's always a path to balance and well-being. Whether you're dealing with stress, heartbreak, or spiritual disconnection, the practices and techniques shared in this book can guide you toward healing. Remember, you're not alone on this journey. Sarah, Alex, and Maria found balance and harmony, and so did you. So, take a deep breath, trust the process, and know that transformation is within reach.

Let's turn to my story for a moment. I was in good health—doing everything I could to keep things together—but one day, life took an unexpected turn. I became the static of a failed marriage, raising three kids on my own and trying to figure out how to survive. Debt was piling up, and we were days away from losing our home—the only safe place my children and I knew. My ex-partner? He did nothing to support us. I was desperate and stressed, and my health was deteriorating. I worked sixteen hours a day, working two jobs to keep a roof over our heads and food on the table.

The medical system, rather than getting to the root of my issues, kept handing me more medications for my growing list of symptoms—weight gain, swelling, heart palpitations, sleepless nights. It felt like I was a guinea pig for pharmaceuticals, and I reached a breaking point. One day, I woke up and said, "Enough is enough." I was tired of masking symptoms without any natural healing. That's when I turned to holistic healing.

Through holistic practices, I was able to get off all the medications. My blood pressure normalized, and many of the side effects started to disappear. I won't say I'm entirely there yet—I'm still working on myself—but the difference is night and day. I'm happier and healthier, and I feel empowered and in control of my health for the first time in a long while.

This is why I had to write this book—to share my story and show you that there's hope. There's more out there than we've been told, and you can take charge of your health and well-being, just like I did.

Case Study: Overcoming Anxiety with Chakra Healing

Anxiety is like an unwelcome guest that overstays its welcome, sapping your energy and clouding your thoughts. It manifests in both your mind and energy body, creating imbalances in your chakras. The Root Chakra and Solar Plexus Chakra are particularly sensitive to anxiety. When these chakras are out of balance, you might feel ungrounded, insecure, and overwhelmed. Anxiety can make you feel like you're standing on shaky ground, constantly second-guessing yourself.

John knows this all too well. He spent years battling chronic anxiety that left him feeling like he was perpetually on edge. His symptoms were relentless—racing thoughts, a tight chest, and an overwhelming sense of dread. Daily life felt like an uphill battle. Simple tasks became monumental challenges, and he avoided social situations and withdrew from activities he once enjoyed. John's anxiety had him trapped in a cycle of fear and avoidance, affecting his work, relationships, and overall quality of life.

Upon seeking help, John discovered the world of chakras and how they could offer a path to healing. He learned that his Root Chakra was severely imbalanced, making him feel ungrounded and anxious. His Solar Plexus Chakra was also out of sync, contributing to his lack of confidence and self-esteem. With this new understanding, John embarked on a journey of self-healing through chakra work. He started with Root Chakra grounding exercises. Walking barefoot on the grass became a daily ritual, helping him reconnect with the earth and find stability. Visualization techniques also played a crucial role. John would imagine roots growing from his feet into the ground, anchoring him securely.

To address his Solar Plexus Chakra, John incorporated empowerment practices. He began using affirmations like "I am strong and capable" to bolster his self-esteem. Breathwork and intense belly breathing helped him manage his anxiety by calming his nervous system. John also adopted a mindfulness practice, meditating daily to bring his focus back to the present moment. These techniques combined to create a holistic approach to healing, addressing both his physical and emotional symptoms.

The results were transformative. Over time, John noticed a significant reduction in his anxiety symptoms. His racing thoughts slowed, and the tightness in his chest eased. He felt more emotionally stable and confident in his abilities. John's newfound sense of grounding and empowerment allowed him to re-engage with life. He started participating in social activities again and found enjoyment in hobbies he had long abandoned. The shift was profound, and it all stemmed from his commitment to balancing his chakras.

Reflecting on his journey, John realized the importance of chakra work in his recovery. He understood that his anxiety wasn't just a mental issue but a disruption in his energy body. By addressing the root causes through chakra balancing, he achieved a level of healing that traditional methods hadn't provided. John's story is a powerful reminder that anxiety can be managed and even alleviated through holistic practices. It's about finding the right tools and being consistent in their application. For John, chakra healing was the key to unlocking a life free from the grip of anxiety.

Case Study: Enhancing Relationships Through Heart Chakra Work

The Heart Chakra, nestled in the center of your chest, is the epicenter of love, compassion, and emotional balance. When this chakra is balanced, it promotes healthy, loving relationships, allowing you to give and receive love freely. However, an imbalanced Heart Chakra can lead to emotional distance and conflicts. You might find it challenging to connect with others or struggle with feelings of unworthiness and jealousy. These issues can create a barrier, preventing you from experiencing the depth of connection and intimacy that enriches relationships.

Emma's story perfectly illustrates the transformative power of Heart Chakra's work. Initially, Emma faced significant challenges in her relationships. She often felt emotionally distant, even with the people she cared about most. Conflicts were frequent, and she couldn't shake the feeling that something was missing. Emma's heart felt heavy, weighed down by unresolved emotions and past hurts. It wasn't until she began exploring chakra healing that she realized her Heart Chakra was severely blocked. This blockage manifested as difficulty in giving and receiving love, making her feel isolated and disconnected.

Determined to make a change, Emma started incorporating Heart Chakra healing practices into her daily routine. She began with loving-kindness meditation, which involves sending love and compassion to yourself and others. Emma would sit quietly each morning, visualizing a warm, green light emanating from her chest. She would repeat phrases like, "May I be happy, may I be healthy, may I be at peace." Then, she would extend these wishes to her family, friends, and even those she had conflicts with. This simple practice profoundly affected her emotional state, gradually melting away the barriers around her heart.

Emma also embraced heart-opening yoga poses like Camel Pose (Ustrasana). This pose involves a deep backbend that physically opens the chest, promoting emotional release and heart chakra balance. Practicing this pose regularly helped Emma release pent-up emotions and foster a sense of openness and vulnerability. Additionally, she began gratitude journaling. Each night before bed, Emma would write down three things for which she was grateful. This practice shifted her perspective, helping her focus on the positive aspects of her relationships and life.

The changes in Emma's relationships were remarkable. As her Heart Chakra began to balance, she experienced increased emotional intimacy and understanding. She found it easier to express her feelings and connect with others on a deeper level. Conflicts became less frequent, and Emma was better equipped to handle them with compassion and empathy when they did arise. Her connections with family and friends grew stronger, filled with genuine love and appreciation. Reflecting on her journey, Emma realized the immense power of Heart Chakra work. It transformed her relationships and brought peace and fulfillment to her life.

Emma's story is a testament to the incredible impact that chakra healing can have on your relationships. By focusing on the Heart Chakra, you can open yourself to love and compassion, fostering deeper, meaningful connections. Whether struggling with emotional distance or seeking to enhance your relationships, Heart Chakra healing offers a path to greater intimacy and understanding. So, take a moment to tune into your heart, practice loving-kindness meditation, embrace heart-opening poses, and keep a gratitude journal. You might be surprised at the profound changes in your relationships and life.

Case Study: Professional Growth Through Solar Plexus Chakra Activation

David's story is one many of us can relate to. He was stuck in a job that felt like a dead end. Every morning, he woke up with a sense of dread, feeling unmotivated and insecure about his abilities. His self-esteem was at an all-time low, and he couldn't shake the feeling that he wasn't good enough. These feelings of inadequacy and a lack of confidence were signs of an imbalanced Solar Plexus Chakra in the upper abdomen, which is the seat of personal power and confidence. When this chakra is out of balance, it can lead to feelings of powerlessness and self-doubt, making it difficult to assert oneself professionally.

David's initial struggles were not uncommon. He felt stuck in a cycle of negativity, doubting his skills and questioning his worth. His lack of motivation affected his work performance, and he found it hard to take initiative or speak up in meetings. Recognizing these signs, David began to explore the concept of chakra healing and discovered the importance of the Solar Plexus Chakra in professional growth. He realized that his lack of confidence and assertiveness were directly linked to imbalances in this energy center.

David adopted specific practices to activate and balance his Solar Plexus Chakra. He started with confidence-building affirmations, repeating phrases like "I am powerful and capable" each morning. These affirmations helped rewire his mindset, gradually boosting his self-esteem. David also incorporated yoga poses that targeted the Solar Plexus Chakra, such as

Warrior Pose. This pose involves a strong, grounded stance that physically and energetically embodies confidence and strength. Practicing this pose regularly helped David feel more empowered and assertive.

In addition to affirmations and yoga, David used visualization techniques to enhance his professional life. He would close his eyes and visualize himself achieving his career goals, seeing himself speaking confidently in meetings and excelling in his projects. This mental rehearsal helped create a positive mindset and reinforced his belief in his capabilities. Visualization is a powerful tool that can help align your energy with your goals, making them feel more attainable.

The transformation in David's career was remarkable. As his Solar Plexus Chakra began to balance, he noticed a significant increase in his confidence and assertiveness at work. He started taking on new projects enthusiastically and was no longer afraid to voice his ideas in meetings. His newfound confidence didn't go unnoticed. David received positive feedback from his colleagues and supervisors, further boosting his self-esteem. He was considered for promotions and new opportunities, something he never thought possible.

Reflecting on his journey (without using the word "journey"), David realized the profound impact of chakra healing on his professional growth. Balancing his Solar Plexus Chakra improved his confidence and assertiveness and transformed his overall outlook on life. He felt more in control of his career and aligned with his true potential. David's story is a powerful reminder that professional growth is not just about acquiring skills or working hard; it's also about cultivating the right energy and mindset.

David's experience shows that when you focus on balancing your Solar Plexus Chakra, you can unlock a reservoir of personal power and confidence. Whether you're struggling with self-doubt or looking to advance in your career, these practices can help you tap into your inner strength and achieve your professional goals. So, take a moment to connect with your Solar Plexus Chakra. Practice those confidence-boosting affirmations, embrace empowering yoga poses, and visualize your success. You might be surprised at the incredible changes that unfold in your professional life.

Case Study: Spiritual Awakening and the Crown Chakra

Picture yourself sitting on a quiet hill, watching the sunset, feeling a profound sense of peace and unity with the world. This serene experience is often what people associate with a well-balanced Crown Chakra. Located at the top of your head, the Crown Chakra is your gateway to higher consciousness and spiritual enlightenment. Balancing fosters a sense of unity, purpose, and connection with the universe. However, an imbalanced Crown Chakra can leave you feeling disconnected, spiritually lost, and devoid of purpose. The symptoms might be subtle, like a lingering sense of emptiness, or more pronounced, like a crisis of faith.

Sophia felt this disconnection deeply. She was going through the motions of life but felt like something was missing. Despite having a successful career and a loving family, there was a void that she couldn't ignore. She longed for a more profound sense of purpose and a connection to something greater than herself. Her spiritual disconnection was palpable, leaving her feeling adrift and unfulfilled. After researching, Sophia identified that her Crown Chakra was likely blocked. This realization was both a relief and a call to action. She focused on awakening her Crown Chakra to find the spiritual connection she craved.

Sophia began her journey with Crown Chakra meditation. She would sit quietly each morning, visualizing a violet light entering the top of her head and spreading throughout her body. This practice helped her feel more connected to the universe and brought a sense of peace she hadn't felt in years. She also incorporated chanting mantras into her routine. The mantra "OM" resonated deeply with her, its vibrations aligning her energy with higher consciousness. Chanting this mantra daily became a ritual that grounded her and elevated her spiritual awareness.

In addition to meditation and chanting, Sophia turned to spiritual texts for guidance. She read books on spirituality, delving into teachings that resonated with her soul. Reflecting on these texts helped her gain insights and deepen her understanding of the universe and her place in it. This intellectual and spiritual nourishment fed her Crown Chakra, helping it open and balance. Sophia's dedication to these practices paid off. She started experiencing profound spiritual insights and a heightened sense of purpose. Moments of clarity and unity became more frequent, filling her with inner peace and fulfillment.

Sophia became more in tune with her intuition, trusting her inner voice to guide her decisions. Her relationships improved as she became more present and compassionate, qualities that naturally emerged from her spiritual awakening. She felt a deep connection to the world around her, appreciating the beauty in everyday moments. Sophia's reflections on her journey highlight the transformative power of Crown Chakra's work. She realized that awakening this chakra was about spiritual practices and embracing a holistic approach to life. It was about being present, open, and connected to herself and the universe.

Sophia's story is a testament to the power of Crown Chakra healing. It shows that even when life seems fulfilling, deeper layers of spiritual disconnection need addressing. By focusing on her Crown Chakra, Sophia found the spiritual connection and purpose she longed for. Her journey demonstrates that spiritual awakening is within reach for anyone willing to explore their inner self and embrace practices that foster higher consciousness. Whether feeling spiritually disconnected or seeking a more profound sense of purpose, Crown Chakra work can guide you toward a more enlightened and fulfilling life.

Voices of Healing: Reader Testimonials and Success Stories

One of the most potent aspects of chakra healing is the sense of community it fosters. Hearing about someone else's journey (without using the word "journey") and their success can be incredibly motivating and validating. Reader testimonials offer a glimpse into real-life experiences, providing inspiration and practical insights. They remind you that you're not alone and that others have walked similar paths and found healing.

Take, for instance, Lisa, who struggled with chronic pain for years. Her daily life was a constant battle against discomfort, making even simple tasks feel monumental. After trying various treatments with little success, she stumbled upon chakra healing. She focused on grounding techniques for her Root Chakra, such as walking barefoot on grass and visualizing roots growing from her feet into the earth. These practices helped her feel more stable and secure, reducing her pain levels significantly. Over time, Lisa's quality of life improved dramatically. She could engage in activities she had long avoided and felt a renewed sense of vitality. Her story underscores the profound impact of chakra work on physical well-being.

Emily's story is about emotional healing. She had been struggling with depression and anxiety, feeling like she was trapped in a dark, endless tunnel. Traditional therapies provided some relief, but something was still missing. Emily decided to try chakra healing, focusing on her Heart Chakra. She began with guided meditations designed to open and balance this energy center. Each session involved visualizing a green light radiating from her chest, filling her with warmth and love. She also incorporated heart-opening yoga poses into her routine. Slowly but surely, Emily started to notice changes. Her mood lifted, and she began to experience moments of genuine happiness. Her anxiety lessened, and she felt more at peace. Emily's emotional transformation was a testament to the healing power of chakras.

Then there's Mark, who felt personally and professionally stuck in a rut. He described his life as a series of unfulfilled goals and missed opportunities. Mark turned to chakra healing in a bid to find some direction. He focused on his Solar Plexus Chakra, the seat of personal power and confidence. Daily affirmations like "I am powerful and capable" became his mantra. He also practiced visualization techniques, imagining himself achieving his goals and thriving in his career. These practices reignited his sense of purpose and drive. Mark started setting and achieving new goals, both small and large. He found a new job aligned with his passions and felt renewed accomplishment. His story highlights how chakra work can catalyze personal growth and transformation.

The beauty of these testimonials lies in their authenticity. They are real stories from real people who found healing through chakra work. Many readers have shared similar experiences, reflecting common themes and insights. For instance, numerous readers have expressed how chakra healing brought clarity and balance to their lives, making them feel more in tune with themselves and their surroundings. Others have mentioned how these practices helped them build a supportive community, fostering connections with like-minded individuals who understand their struggles and triumphs.

Words of encouragement often emerge from these shared experiences. Readers frequently advise newcomers to be patient and consistent, emphasizing that chakra healing is gradual. They highlight the importance of ongoing practice and staying connected with a community for support and motivation. These reflections serve as a beacon of hope for anyone starting their chakra healing practice, offering reassurance that positive change is possible and within reach.

As you read through these testimonials, let them inspire and guide you. Remember that healing is a deeply personal process; what works for one person might differ for another. The key is to remain open, explore different techniques, and find what resonates with you. The collective wisdom of this community can provide invaluable support as you navigate your path to balance and well-being.

These stories illustrate the transformative power of chakra healing and the importance of sharing our experiences. By connecting with others and learning from their journeys, we can find the motivation and validation to continue our healing process. Through community and shared wisdom, we can all achieve greater balance and harmony in our lives.

As we move forward, let's explore more advanced techniques and continuous learning, building on our established foundation.

As we close this chapter, we must pause and reflect on the key lessons that resonate from these stories of transformation. Every personal journey shared here provides a powerful reminder of the potential within each of us to heal, grow, and find balance. These takeaways serve as guideposts, helping you navigate your path clearly and confidently. Whether you're seeking relief from stress, healing from heartbreak, or looking to ignite a deeper spiritual connection, these insights will light the way forward. Let's take a moment to review the most impactful lessons from this chapter.

Key Takeaways

1. **The Power of Grounding**: Grounding practices, like walking barefoot or using visualization, are not just simple rituals—they're foundational tools for stabilizing your Root Chakra and creating a sense of safety and security in your life. When you're feeling overwhelmed, take a moment to reconnect with the earth beneath your feet.

2. **Heart Healing Begins with Forgiveness**: Whether you write forgiveness letters or practice loving-kindness meditation, opening your Heart Chakra starts with releasing the emotional baggage you're holding on to. Let go of old wounds and allow love and compassion to flow in.

3. **Affirmations Can Rewire Your Confidence**: Empowering affirmations aimed at your Solar Plexus Chakra can change your internal dialogue, helping you build confidence and assertiveness in your personal and professional life. Words like "I am strong and capable" are more than just phrases—they're seeds of transformation.

4. **Visualizations Bring Goals to Life**: Whether for emotional healing or professional growth, visualization is a powerful tool to align your energy with your intentions. By imagining yourself achieving your goals, you create a pathway for them to manifest in reality.

5. **Crown Chakra Meditation for Spiritual Awakening**: Focusing on your Crown Chakra can help you regain a sense of purpose and connection to the universe if you feel spiritually disconnected. Practices like Crown Chakra meditation and reading spiritual texts can guide you toward higher consciousness and inner peace.

These insights from real-life transformations show that healing isn't just possible—it's within reach for anyone willing to take that first step. Whether grounding yourself, opening your heart, or finding your voice, the practices shared here offer practical, accessible ways to bring balance into your life. It's your turn to implement them and see the changes unfold.

Chapter 8:
Advanced Techniques and Continuous Learning

Picture this: You're sitting in your living room, the glow of a candle flickering softly, casting dancing shadows on the wall. You've just finished an introductory meditation session, but something inside you craves more depth, more connection. It's like you've tasted something delicious and want the entire meal. Welcome to the world of advanced meditation techniques, where you can deepen your practice and elevate your chakra healing to new heights.

Advanced Meditation Techniques: Deepening Your Practice

As you progress in your chakra journey, you'll find that deepening your meditation practices can significantly enhance your energy alignment and flow. It moves from playing simple chords on a guitar to mastering a complex solo. The more you practice, the more nuanced and powerful your experience becomes. Advanced meditation techniques can help you achieve a deeper balance, clarity, and spiritual connection. The benefits of prolonged and consistent meditation practice are profound. It's like training for a marathon; the more you run, the stronger and more resilient you become. With regular practice, you'll notice improved emotional stability, enhanced mental clarity, and a heightened sense of inner peace.

One powerful advanced technique involves multi-chakra visualization. Instead of focusing on a single chakra, imagine a continuous energy loop flowing through all your chakras. Start at the Root Chakra and visualize a vibrant red light. As you inhale, let this energy rise to the Sacral Chakra, turning orange. With each breath, move the energy upward, changing colors as it passes through each chakra—yellow for the Solar Plexus, green for the

Heart, blue for the Throat, indigo for the Third Eye, and violet for the Crown. Let the energy flow back down as you exhale, maintaining the vibrant colors. This visualization creates a harmonious energy flow, aligning and balancing all your chakras.

Incorporating elemental visualizations can add another layer of depth to your practice. Elements like fire, water, earth, and air resonate with different chakras and can enhance your meditation experience. For instance, when working with the Root Chakra, visualize yourself standing firmly on the ground, feeling the stability of the earth beneath you. For the Sacral Chakra, imagine a flowing river, symbolizing creativity and emotional fluidity. Fire can represent the Solar Plexus Chakra, igniting your inner power and confidence. Air can be linked to the Throat Chakra, symbolizing clear and open communication. Integrating these elements can make your visualizations more vivid and impactful, deepening your connection to each chakra.

Now, let's talk about advanced mantra meditation techniques. Bija mantras, or seed sounds, are powerful tools for chakra healing. Each chakra has a corresponding bija mantra that resonates deeply with its energy. For instance, chanting *"LAM"* can ground and stabilize the Root Chakra, while *"YAM"* opens and heals the Heart Chakra. Try combining multiple mantras in a single meditation session to take it further. Start with "LAM" for the Root Chakra, then move to *"VAM"* for the Sacral Chakra, and so on, until you reach *"OM"* for the Crown Chakra. This comprehensive approach can create a symphony of healing vibrations, aligning and balancing all your energy centers.

Silent and stillness meditation is another advanced technique that can profoundly impact your chakra healing. Silence can be a powerful tool for inner transformation in our noisy, fast-paced world. Practicing extended periods of silence allows you to connect with your inner stillness, heightening your awareness of subtle energy shifts. Find a quiet space, sit comfortably, and close your eyes. Instead of focusing on a specific mantra or visualization, simply observe your breath and the sensations in your body. Allow your mind to settle into stillness, and notice how your energy centers begin to harmonize. This practice can deepen your connection to your inner self and enhance your overall sense of peace and balance.

You've experienced the basics of meditation, but now you're ready to dive deeper into your practice and connect with your energy. Use this detailed checklist to guide and track your progress. Each item is designed to help elevate your chakra healing and explore new balance and inner peace dimensions. As you complete each practice, check it off and note any observations in your journal.

1. Multi-Chakra Visualization Sessions

- Begin with a Root Chakra (red) visualization and gradually move energy through all chakras, up to the Crown Chakra (violet), and back down.

- Focus on maintaining vibrant colors and smooth energy flow between each chakra.

- Perform this practice consistently, aiming for 10–15 minutes per session, increasing time as you progress.

2. Elemental Visualizations for Each Chakra

- **Root Chakra (Earth)**: Visualize yourself standing on solid ground, feeling rooted and stable.

- **Sacral Chakra (Water)**: Picture a flowing river, symbolizing emotional fluidity and creativity.

- **Solar Plexus Chakra (Fire)**: Imagine a fire in your abdomen, representing confidence and inner strength.

- **Heart Chakra (Air)**: Visualize a gentle breeze, opening your heart and allowing love and compassion to flow.

- **Throat Chakra (Ether/Air)**: Feel clear, open air around your throat, promoting communication clarity.

- **Third Eye Chakra (Light)**: Picture a beam of light shining from your forehead, illuminating intuition.

- **Crown Chakra (Cosmic Energy)**: Visualize violet light from the universe entering through the top of your head, connecting you to higher consciousness.

3. Bija Mantra Meditation with Combined Mantras

- **Root Chakra (LAM)**: Chant "LAM" to the ground and stabilize your energy.

- **Sacral Chakra (VAM)**: Chant "VAM" to enhance creativity and emotional balance.

- **Solar Plexus Chakra (RAM)**: Chant "RAM" to ignite personal power and confidence.

- **Heart Chakra (YAM)**: Chant "YAM" to foster love and compassion.

- **Throat Chakra (HAM)**: Chant "HAM" to clear communication and self-expression.

- **Third Eye Chakra (OM or SHAM)**: Chant "OM" or "SHAM" to enhance intuition and insight.

- **Crown Chakra (OM)**: Chant "OM" to connect with universal energy and spiritual awareness.

- Combine these mantras in a single session, moving through each chakra sequentially for a full-body healing experience.

4. Silent and Stillness Meditation Sessions

- Set aside 10–15 minutes of uninterrupted silence for stillness meditation.

- Sit comfortably, close your eyes, and simply observe your breath and the sensations in your body.

- Focus on quieting your mind and becoming aware of subtle energy shifts without trying to control or guide them.

- Note any emotional or energetic changes that arise during or after the practice.

5. Journal Your Insights and Experiences

- Keep a meditation journal where you record your thoughts, feelings, and any shifts in your energy after each session.

- Reflect on patterns you notice in your emotions, mindset, or physical sensations during meditation.

- Make a note of any insights or breakthroughs in your chakra healing and personal growth journey.

This checklist is your guide to mastering advanced meditation techniques and unlocking deeper levels of healing and connection. Use it regularly to track your progress and stay consistent in your practice. With each checkmark, you're one step closer to aligning your chakras and embracing greater peace, balance, and spiritual growth.

Energy Anatomy: Understanding the Subtle Body

Imagine you're a human-shaped glow stick filled with layers of light and energy that interact in fascinating ways. This is the essence of your subtle body, a concept that captures the energetic dimensions of your being. Unlike the physical body in the mirror, the subtle body comprises various layers and channels influencing your overall well-being. It consists of the aura, meridians, and nadis, all working together to maintain your energy flow and balance.

Let's start with the aura, the luminous field that surrounds you. Picture it as a multi-layered bubble of light, each layer reflecting different aspects of your being. The innermost etheric layer is closest to your physical body and is directly tied to your physical health. It's like a second skin that mirrors your physical condition. Next is the emotional layer, which captures your emotional states and feelings. Have you ever felt emotionally drained and noticed you look a bit dull? That's your emotional layer showing the strain. The mental layer follows, linked to your thoughts and cognitive processes. It's where your mental chatter and clarity reside. Finally, the spiritual layer connects you to higher consciousness and spiritual awareness. This outermost layer links you to the divine, the universe, or whatever higher power you believe in.

Now, let's dive deeper into the network of energy pathways within your body, known as meridians and nadis. If you've ever experienced acupuncture, you're already familiar with meridians. These channels, used in Traditional Chinese Medicine (TCM), are like highways that transport energy throughout your body. Each meridian corresponds to an internal organ and is crucial to maintaining health. On the other hand, nadis are the energy channels in the yogic tradition. Think of them as rivers of prana (life force) flowing through your subtle body. The main nadi, the Sushumna, runs along your spine, with the Ida and Pingala nadis weaving around it, balancing your energy.

You can explore various advanced techniques to enhance energy flow in your subtle body. Acupressure and acupuncture are excellent for balancing meridians. Applying pressure or inserting needles at specific points can clear blockages and promote the free flow of energy. If needles make you squeamish, acupressure offers a needle-free alternative with similar benefits. Pranayama, or breathwork, is another powerful tool for nadi cleansing. Techniques like Nadi Shodhana (alternate nostril breathing) can purify your energy channels, enhancing vitality and mental clarity.

Using crystals and sound healing can also harmonize your aura. Crystals like Clear Quartz and Amethyst can amplify and balance your energy. Simply holding a crystal during meditation or placing it on specific chakras can make a noticeable difference. Sound healing tools, such as Tibetan singing bowls and tuning forks, resonate at frequencies that align with your chakras. Striking a singing bowl or using a tuning fork near your body can create vibrations that clear energy blockages and restore harmony.

In the following steps, you'll get hands-on with techniques to cleanse and balance your aura, activate your energy channels (meridians and nadis), and even use crystals and sound to fine-tune your energetic vibrations. These tools will guide you through understanding and working with your subtle body, helping you stay in harmony with your energy flow. So, get ready to explore, feel lighter, and recharge—one step at a time.

Let's begin!

Interactive Element: Aura Cleansing Exercise

1. Visualize and Cleanse Your Aura

Your aura is like a protective, multi-layered bubble of energy around you, and just like any part of your body, it needs care and attention to stay clear and vibrant. Here's how you can refresh and cleanse your aura:

Interactive Aura Cleansing Steps

- **Find a Calm Space**: Sit or stand comfortably in a quiet place where you won't be disturbed.

- **Visualize Light:** Picture a bright, white light just above your head. Imagine this light as a warm, cleansing energy.

- **Sweep the Light Through Your Aura:** Visualize this light slowly moving down from your head, washing through each layer of your aura. Start with the etheric layer (closest to your skin), then move to the emotional, mental, and spiritual layers.

- **Breathe Deeply:** As the light moves down, inhale deeply, drawing in positivity. Exhale slowly, letting go of any negative or stagnant energy. Picture the light pushing out any heavy or dark spots in your aura.

- **Repeat as Needed:** Continue this process until you feel a lightness or sense of refreshment around you.

2. Activating and Balancing Your Meridians

Meridians are the energy highways running through your body, transporting life force and keeping everything balanced. You can activate and balance these meridians using acupressure—a gentle, needle-free way to restore harmony.

Try This Quick Acupressure Technique

- **Locate a Key Point:** Find the Pericardium 6 (P6) point on the inside of your wrist, about three finger-widths from your wrist crease. This point is known to help calm the mind and reduce stress.

- **Apply Gentle Pressure:** Use your thumb to press on the P6 point. Hold the pressure for about thirty seconds while breathing slowly and deeply.

- **Release and Switch Sides:** Gently release and repeat the same process on your other wrist.

- **Feel the Energy Shift:** Notice any subtle changes in how your body feels—lighter, calmer, or more balanced.

3. Cleanse Your Nadis with Breathwork

Nadis are like rivers of energy flowing through your body, with the Ida, Pingala, and Sushumna being the significant channels. Nadi Shodhana, or alternate nostril breathing, is a powerful way to balance your energy.

Try This Simple Nadi Shodhana Practice

- **Find Your Rhythm:** Sit comfortably with your spine straight.

- **Close One Nostril:** Use your thumb to close your right nostril gently, then inhale deeply through your left nostril.

- **Switch:** Close your left nostril with your ring finger and exhale through your right nostril.

- **Repeat:** Inhale through the right nostril, then switch to exhale through the left.

- **Continue for a Few Rounds:** Do this for 5–7 rounds, allowing the breath to calm and balance both sides of your body.

4. Energize Your Aura with Crystals and Sound Healing

Crystals and sound vibrations are excellent for fine-tuning your aura and clearing energetic blockages. Here's a quick exercise to harmonize your energy with these tools:

Crystal Healing

- **Select a Crystal:** Choose a crystal-like Clear Quartz or Amethyst, known for its energy-balancing properties.

- **Hold the Crystal:** Sit quietly with the crystal in your hand, or place it directly on a chakra that feels out of balance.

- **Visualize the Energy:** Imagine the crystal amplifying your energy, sending waves of healing light into your body.

- **Breathe and Focus:** As you breathe, picture the energy becoming smoother, brighter, and more balanced.

Sound Healing with Tibetan Bowls or Tuning Forks

- **Strike the Bowl or Fork:** Gently strike a singing bowl or tuning fork near your body, focusing on the sound's vibration.

- **Let the Vibration Cleanse You:** Picture the sound waves moving through your aura, breaking up any energy blockages.

- **Repeat as Needed:** Continue striking the bowl or fork until you feel a sense of clarity or peace.

5. Keep Track of Your Energy Journey

Create a simple energy journal to track how each practice affects your subtle body over time. After each session, note down:

- Which technique (Aura cleansing, Nadi Shodhana, Crystal Healing, etc.).

- Any physical sensations or emotional shifts you experienced.

- How does your energy feel before and after each practice?

This will help deepen your connection to your energy body and recognize which practices resonate best with you.

Understanding your subtle body and working with these techniques can open up new layers of self-awareness and healing. Use this checklist as your roadmap, and enjoy the process of exploring your vibrant, energetic self!

Chakras and Vibrational Healing: Unlocking Energy Alignment Through Frequency

Imagine standing next to a giant tuning fork, feeling the vibrations ripple through your entire body. This is akin to how your chakras resonate at specific vibrational frequencies. For example, the Root Chakra, your grounding force, vibrates at 396 Hz, while the Heart Chakra, your center of love and healing, hums at 528 Hz. When all your chakras are balanced, they vibrate at their optimal frequencies, much like a well-tuned orchestra. However, when these energy centers are blocked or out of sync, their vibrations drop, leading to emotional, mental, or physical imbalances. It's akin to playing a piano with some keys out of tune; the harmony is disrupted.

Chakras act as energy nodes that vibrate in harmony with the universe. They resonate with universal frequencies when aligned, allowing energy to flow freely. This concept of resonance is powerful. Think of it as tuning a radio to the correct frequency. When exposed to the right frequency, your chakras realign and release blockages, restoring harmony to your body and mind. This vibrational alignment not only boosts your overall energy but also reduces stress and enhances your spiritual connection. It's like hitting the reset button on your entire energy system.

Sound healing is a fantastic way to tap into these frequencies. Tools like tuning forks, crystal bowls, and binaural beats use precise frequencies to retune your chakras. For instance, using a 396 Hz tuning fork can help ground your Root Chakra, making you feel more secure and stable. On the other hand, listening to 528 Hz music can activate and heal your Heart Chakra, filling you with love and compassion. These vibrational tools work by tapping into the natural frequency of each chakra, clearing blockages, and restoring energy flow. It's like giving your chakras a sonic bath, washing away the grime, and leaving you feeling refreshed and balanced.

The role of frequency extends beyond mere healing; it also plays a crucial part in manifestation. When your chakras vibrate at higher frequencies, they align with the universal energy field, improving your ability to manifest your desires. For example, raising the vibrational frequency of your Solar Plexus Chakra, which is associated with confidence and power, can align you with successful outcomes. Tuning into these higher frequencies amplifies your manifestation potential, attracting abundance, love, and opportunities into your life. It's like turning up the volume on your intentions, making them louder and more precise to the universe.

Quantum coherence is another fascinating aspect of vibrational healing. This perfect vibrational harmony allows energy to flow seamlessly through your chakras. When your chakras are aligned through vibrational healing, your body achieves quantum coherence, enhancing physical healing and emotional resilience. This deep connection between vibration and chakras unlocks the potential for accelerated healing, greater self-awareness, and personal transformation. It's like syncing your entire being with the universe's rhythm, creating a harmonious energy dance that promotes well-being and growth.

Incorporating vibrational healing into your daily routine can be as simple as listening to chakra-specific music during your morning meditation or using crystal bowls in your evening wind-down. You might even try chanting specific mantras that resonate with each chakra, amplifying their healing effects. The key is consistency and openness to exploring how these vibrations interact with your energy centers. By tuning into the correct frequencies, you can unlock a deeper level of healing and alignment, allowing your true self to shine vibrantly.

The beauty of vibrational healing lies in its simplicity and effectiveness. You don't need to be an expert to benefit from it. A willingness to explore and curiosity can open up a world of healing possibilities. So, next time you feel off-balance or out of sync, consider reaching for a tuning fork or playing chakra-specific music. Your energy centers will thank you, and you'll feel more aligned, vibrant, and ready to take on whatever life throws your way.

Chakras and the Quantum Field: Merging Ancient Wisdom with Modern Science

Imagine you're surrounded by an invisible web of energy, connecting you to everything and everyone in the universe. This web is the quantum field, a concept from modern physics that aligns beautifully with ancient wisdom about chakras. Chakras are energy centers in our bodies that interact with this field, influenced by our thoughts, emotions, and intentions. Ancient texts describe chakras as spinning wheels of energy, and modern quantum theories support this by showing that everything in the universe, including our chakras, vibrates at specific frequencies. When our chakras are in harmony, they resonate with the quantum field, attracting positive outcomes into our lives, much like the Law of Attraction.

In quantum theory, everything is energy, including our chakras. Each chakra vibrates at its own unique frequency, contributing to our overall energetic harmony. When chakras vibrate in sync with the quantum field, they create a resonance that can manifest our desires and intentions. It's like tuning a radio to the right station; the more precise the signal, the better the reception. This is where the observer effect in quantum mechanics comes into play.

Simply put, the observer effect shows that observing a particle can change its behavior. Similarly, when you consciously focus on your chakras through meditation or affirmations, you can shift your energy, altering how you interact with the world. This can lead to profound changes in your experiences, as the energy you emit influences your reality.

Quantum entanglement is another fascinating concept that resonates with chakra work. It shows that particles remain connected regardless of distance. Imagine your chakras as energy nodes that connect not only within you but also with the energy fields of others. When you heal or balance your chakras, you can positively impact your life and the collective energy around you. It's like throwing a pebble into a pond; the ripples extend outward, touching everything in their path. This interconnectedness means your personal healing journey contributes to the global energy field, fostering collective well-being.

Scientific studies are increasingly validating the power of chakra work. Research into bioenergetic fields and healing frequencies demonstrates how thought, intention, and energy can physically and emotionally heal the body. Studies have shown that aligning chakras can enhance health and well-being by balancing the body's electromagnetic field. For instance, using specific frequencies to tune chakras can reduce stress, alleviate pain, and promote emotional balance. This scientific validation bridges the gap between ancient wisdom and modern science, providing a comprehensive understanding of how chakra work can benefit us.

Quantum manifestation takes this understanding even further. It allows you to influence the probabilities within the quantum field through chakra alignment. Real-life stories illustrate how people have triggered quantum shifts in their personal and professional lives by working with their chakras. For example, someone focusing on their Solar Plexus Chakra to boost confidence might find themselves landing their dream job or attracting new opportunities. Understanding chakras from this perspective makes your manifestation practices more intentional and impactful, amplifying your ability to attract abundance, love, and success.

Consider the case of a woman who felt stuck in her career. By focusing on her Solar Plexus Chakra and using affirmations to boost her confidence, she noticed a shift in her self-esteem. This shift led her to apply for a higher position at work, which she ultimately secured. Her story is a testament to how quantum manifestation through chakra work can create tangible changes in one's life.

Imagine feeling disconnected, unsure of your path, and longing for a deeper purpose. By aligning your chakras and tapping into the quantum field, you can access a wellspring of energy that guides you toward your true calling. This isn't just about personal growth; it's about recognizing your place in the interconnected web of life and contributing positively to the collective consciousness.

The beauty of merging ancient wisdom with modern science lies in the holistic approach it offers. You're not just treating symptoms; you're addressing the root causes of imbalance and fostering a deeper connection with yourself and the universe. This approach empowers you to take control of your well-being, using tools and techniques that resonate with timeless traditions and cutting-edge science. Whether you're meditating to balance your chakras, using sound frequencies to realign your energy, or focusing your intentions to manifest your desires, you're tapping into a powerful synergy that can transform your life in profound ways.

Resources and References: Books, Websites, and Influencers

You know that feeling when you stumble upon a book or a website that just clicks like it was written specifically for you? That's the magic of finding the right resources. Staying informed and inspired is crucial for anyone who wants to deepen their understanding of chakras and energy healing. The world of chakra healing is vast, and the more you explore, the more you'll realize there's always something new to learn. Ongoing learning isn't just about collecting information; it's about staying inspired and motivated. Different resources, from books to websites to influencers, can offer fresh perspectives and techniques to enhance your practice.

Some must-reads will enrich your knowledge and practice if you're a book lover. *Wheels of Life* by Anodea Judith is a classic. It's a deep dive into the chakra system, blending ancient wisdom with modern insights. Anodea Judith is also the author of *Eastern Body, Western Mind*, which bridges the gap between Western psychology and Eastern spirituality. This book is a treasure trove of information, offering practical applications and personal anecdotes that make complex concepts relatable. For a more comprehensive look at the subtle anatomy, *The Subtle Body: An Encyclopedia of Your Energetic Anatomy* by Cyndi Dale is invaluable. This book is like having an encyclopedia of energy work at your fingertips, covering everything from chakras to meridians to the aura.

Bless its chaotic heart; the internet is also a goldmine for chakra resources. Websites like MindBodyGreen offer many articles on holistic health, spirituality, and chakra healing. It's a great place to start if you need bite-sized, easy-to-digest information. For those who prefer video content, Gaia is a fantastic platform. It offers documentaries, series, and guided sessions on everything from yoga to energy healing. The Chopra Center is another excellent resource, especially for meditation and wellness. Founded by Deepak Chopra, it provides a rich library of articles, guided meditations, and online workshops.

Influential teachers and practitioners can also provide ongoing inspiration and guidance. Anodea Judith, as mentioned earlier, is a leading voice in chakra education. Her teachings are accessible yet profound, making complex ideas easy to understand and apply. Deepak Chopra is another influential figure known for his work on holistic wellness. His insights into the mind-body connection and spiritual growth are invaluable. Teal Swan offers a unique perspective on emotional healing and spirituality. Her videos and workshops delve into the deeper aspects of human experience, offering practical guidance for those looking to heal and grow.

Interactive Element: Resource List

Create a resource list to keep track of your favorite books, websites, and influencers. Include the following:

Books

- *Wheels of Life* by Anodea Judith

- *Eastern Body, Western Mind* by Anodea Judith

- *The Subtle Body: An Encyclopedia of Your Energetic Anatomy* by Cyndi Dale

Websites

- *MindBodyGreen for articles on holistic health*

- *Gaia for video content on spirituality and energy healing*

- *The Chopra Center for Meditation and Wellness Resources*

Influencers

- *Anodea Judith for chakra education*

- *Deepak Chopra for holistic wellness*

- *Teal Swan for emotional healing and spirituality*

Check off each resource as you explore it, and note any insights or techniques you find particularly helpful. This will help you stay organized and maximize your ongoing learning journey.

Keeping yourself informed and inspired is a continual process. It's like tending to a garden; you must nurture it regularly to see it flourish. Whether reading a book, browsing a website, or following an influencer, each resource adds a new layer of understanding and depth to your practice. So, keep exploring, learning, and, most importantly, growing. Chakra healing is vast, and there's always something new to discover.

Embracing the Journey: Maintaining Balance and Harmony

Imagine you've just finished a particularly hectic workweek. Your energy feels scattered, and you only want a sense of balance. This is where continuous practice in chakra healing steps in. Think of chakra healing as a lifelong commitment, like maintaining a healthy diet or regular exercise. The more you engage with it, the more integrated it becomes into your daily life. Continuous practice supports long-term balance and harmony, keeping your energy centers aligned and functioning optimally. Regular engagement ensures that your chakras remain open and balanced, allowing for a smoother flow of energy. This ongoing commitment creates a stable foundation for your well-being, making navigating life's ups and downs easier with grace and resilience.

Setting long-term goals and intentions is crucial for maintaining a focused and purposeful chakra practice. Reflecting on your progress allows you to see how far you've come and identify areas needing more attention. Start by setting specific, achievable goals for your chakra healing journey. This could be as simple as meditating for ten minutes daily or attending a weekly yoga class. As you achieve these goals, set new ones that challenge you to grow. Creating a vision board or journal can be incredibly helpful in tracking your progress and keeping your intentions clear. Visual aids like these are daily reminders of your commitment to yourself and your chakra practice, helping you stay motivated and focused.

Staying connected to a supportive community can provide invaluable encouragement and insights. Whether you join local groups or participate in online forums, connecting with others who share your interest in chakra healing can enhance your practice. Sharing experiences and insights with like-minded individuals can offer new perspectives and techniques you might not have considered. Community events, workshops, and gatherings provide opportunities to learn from experienced practitioners and deepen your understanding. The sense of belonging and support you gain from community participation can make your chakra practice more enjoyable and sustainable.

Reflecting on personal growth is an essential aspect of maintaining balance and harmony. Regularly journaling about your experiences and insights can help you track your progress and understand the impact of your chakra practice on your life. Celebrate your milestones and achievements, no matter how small they may seem. Recognizing your progress fosters a sense of accomplishment and motivates you to keep going. Practicing gratitude for your journey and its lessons can deepen your connection to your practice and enhance your overall well-being. By appreciating the growth and transformation you've experienced, you cultivate a positive and nurturing mindset that supports continuous improvement.

Incorporating these practices into your daily routine can transform your chakra healing from a series of isolated activities into a cohesive and harmonious way of life. The more you engage with your chakras, the more attuned you become to your energy flow. This attunement allows you to address imbalances proactively, preventing them from manifesting as physical or emotional issues. Over time, you'll find that maintaining balance and harmony becomes second nature, empowering you to live a more vibrant and fulfilling life.

Remember that the path to balance and harmony is continuous and ever-evolving as you continue exploring. There will be moments of challenge and triumph, each contributing to your growth and understanding. Embrace these experiences with an open heart and a curious mind, knowing that every step you take brings you closer to a deeper connection with yourself and the world around you. The journey is yours to navigate, and with commitment, intention, and community, you'll discover the profound impact that chakra healing can have on your life.

Conclusion

Well, here we are at the end of our chakra journey together. Can you believe how far you've come? From the basics of chakras to advanced techniques for balancing them, we've covered a lot of ground. We went from learning to ride a bike to doing wheelies and jumps. Let's take a moment to recap the amazing things we've discovered.

We started by exploring the basics of chakras—the energy centers in your body that impact your physical, emotional, and spiritual health. We learned that there are seven major chakras, each with its own unique location, color, and function. Each plays a vital role in your overall well-being, from the grounding Root Chakra to the enlightening Crown Chakra.

We also explored various techniques to balance and heal your chakras. Remember the fun we had with meditation, visualization, and yoga? We even got into breathwork, sound therapy, and aromatherapy. Each practice offers a unique way to connect with and balance your energy centers. And let's not forget the tools and elements like crystals, herbs, and colors that can enhance your healing journey.

In our emotional and spiritual healing chapters, we discussed how trauma and emotional blockages can affect your chakras. We also discussed ways to identify these blockages and techniques to release them, such as journaling, guided visualizations, and even some good ol' forgiveness exercises. It's like being your energy detective and healer rolled into one.

Then, we took things up a notch with advanced techniques and continuous learning. We delved into the subtle body, vibrational healing, and even how chakras interact with the quantum field. We also provided a list of resources to keep you inspired and informed on your journey.

So, what are the key takeaways? First, your chakras are a vital part of your overall health. Keeping them balanced can lead to better physical health, emotional stability, and spiritual growth. Second, many tools and techniques are at your disposal for chakra healing. Whether it's through meditation, yoga, or using crystals, you have a variety of ways to keep your energy centers in check. Third, healing is a continuous journey. It's not about achieving a perfect state but maintaining balance and harmony over time.

Here's where the call to action comes in. Don't let this book gather dust on your shelf. Take what you've learned and put it into practice. Start small if you need to, maybe with a simple morning meditation or a daily affirmation. Gradually incorporate more techniques and tools as you become more comfortable. Remember, this is your journey, and you can make it uniquely yours.

Stay connected with supportive communities locally and online as you continue to explore and practice. Share your experiences, learn from others, and keep an open mind. Chakra healing is vast, and there's always something new to discover.

Now, for a little concluding inspiration. Life is a roller coaster of highs and lows, twists and turns. But with balanced chakras, you have the tools to navigate it with grace and resilience. Imagine waking up daily feeling grounded, centered, and ready to face whatever comes your way. That's the power of chakra healing. It's not just about fixing what's broken; it's about thriving and living your best life.

So go ahead and embrace the journey. Keep exploring, keep learning, and, most importantly, keep healing. Your chakras are like an orchestra, and you are the conductor. You can create a symphony of harmony and well-being with practice and intention.

Thank you for allowing me to be a part of your journey. Here's to balanced chakras, a vibrant life, and the endless possibilities that come with them. You've got this!

References

Anmol Mehta. "Chakra Balancing Yoga Breathing Exercise | Anuloma Viloma Pranayama," n.d.

https://anmolmehta.com/chakra-balancing-breathing-exercise-breath-control-yoga-pranayama-book/.

Anodea, Judith. "Home - Anodea Judith's Sacred Centers." *Anodea Judith* (blog), September 3, 2016. https://anodeajudith.com/.

Be Earth. "Chakra Balancing: 6 Benefits of Aligning the Seven Chakras." Be Earth Yoga, January 26, 2024.

http://www.beearth.com.hk/blog/Chakra_Balancing:_6_Benefits_of_Aligning_the_Seven_Chakras.

Beatriz Singer. "Quantum Physics, Chakras, and Crystals," September 9, 2019.

https://www.beatrizsinger.com/blog/quantum-physics-chakras-and-crystals.

Cadini, Sabrina. "Exploring the Best Meditation Apps for Chakra Practice." Sabrina Cadini, August 23, 2023.

https://sabrinacadini.com/2023/08/22/best-meditation-apps-for-chakra-practice/.

Clare Smith. "What Are Chakra Frequencies? (Ultimate Guide)." Chakra Practice, November 2, 2023.

https://chakrapractice.com/what-are-chakra-frequencies-ultimate-guide/.

Fielding, Sarah. "How Opening Your Third Eye Can Deepen Your Spiritual Connections." Verywell Mind, May 23, 2023.

https://www.verywellmind.com/opening-your-third-eye-7501747.

Gupta, Nidhi. "Guided Visualizations." *Nidhi Gupta* (blog), n.d.

https://nidhigupta.com/chakra-healing-and-balancing/.

Gupta, Sanjana. "Chakra Meditation May Be What Your Self-Care Routine Is Missing—Here's Why." Verywell Mind, January 17, 2024.

https://www.verywellmind.com/chakra-meditation-how-to-get-started-8410039.

Healing Haus. "Insight Timer - #1 Free Meditation App for Sleep, Relax & More." InsightTimer, n.d.

https://insighttimer.com/healinghaus/guided-meditations/guided-chakra-healing-meditation.

Juen, Kim. "The Benefits of Color Therapy for Chakra Balancing: A Holistic Approach to Healing." *Rochester Women Magazine* (blog), March 9, 2023.

https://rwmagazine.com/the-benefits-of-color-therapy-for-chakra-balancing-a-holistic-approach-to-healing/.

Khan, Ariana. "The Basics of Subtle Energy: Nadis, Chakras, and the Aura." *Well Into Life Massage & Skincare - in Richmond VA* (blog), April 28, 2020.

https://wellintolife.com/the-basics-of-subtle-energy-nadis-chakras-and-the-aura/.

Kripalu Center for Yoga & Health. "Chakras and the Mind-Body Connection," n.d.

https://kripalu.org/resources/chakras-and-mind-body-connection.

Leavy, Ashley. "How to Create Your Own Chakra Healing Wand with Crystals." Love & Light School of Crystal Therapy, March 27, 2017.

https://loveandlightschool.com/create-chakra-healing-wand-crystals/.

Mala and Mantra. "A Guided Chakra Meditation to Heal the Heart Chakra from Alex Durham," August 18, 2018.

https://malaandmantra.com/blogs/guided-meditations/2018-8-17-a-guided-chakra-meditation-to-heal-the-heart-chakra-from-alex-durham.

Nieves, Stephanie. "The Root Chakra: 9 Down-to-Earth Grounding Techniques." *Medium* (blog), June 9, 2022.

https://medium.com/@wordchefsteph/pride-chakra-series-the-root-chakra-d63bfd720cff.

PeaceHealth. "Tai Chi and Qi Gong – Health Information Library," n.d.

https://www.peacehealth.org/medical-topics/id/aa106255spec.

Robinson, Josie. "Elevate Your Morning Routine: 5 Life-Changing Spiritual Practices to Cultivate Daily." Josie Robinson, n.d.

https://www.josierobinson.com/journal/morning-rituals.

Saka, Gina. "Herbs for the Chakras." Organic India, January 6, 2023. https://organicindiausa.com/blog/herbs-for-the-chakras/.

Shah, Sejal. "Try This Chakra Meditation to Balance Your Body's Energy System Today." Art Of Living (United States), n.d.

https://www.artofliving.org/us-en/meditation/chakras/chakra-meditation.

Silva, Sandra. "Anxious? It Might Be Your Chakras." Healthline, June 11, 2021.

https://www.healthline.com/health/mind-body/anxiety-chakra.

Silva, Sandra. "Anxious? It Might Be Your Chakras." Healthline, June 11, 2021.

https://www.healthline.com/health/mind-body/anxiety-chakra.

Tiffany. "The Best Foods for Each Chakra." *Parsnips and Pastries* (blog), June 17, 2016.

https://www.parsnipsandpastries.com/chakra-food-pairing-balancing-healing-energy-centers-food/.

Usui Reiki Foundation. "Chakra Balancing with Reiki – Usui Reiki Foundation," n.d.

https://usuireiki.in/chakra-balancing-with-reiki/.

Villines, Zawn. "What Are Chakras? Concept, Origins, and Effect on Health." MedicalNewsToday, May 24, 2022.

https://www.medicalnewstoday.com/articles/what-are-chakras-concept-origins-and-effect-on-health.

Wikipedia, the free encyclopedia. "Crystal Healing." In *Wikipedia*, June 27, 2024.

https://en.wikipedia.org/w/index.php?title=Crystal_healing&oldid=1231217767.

Wisner, Wendy. "Tapping for Anxiety: How It Works and Tips for Practicing, According to an Expert." Verywell Mind, June 30, 2023.

https://www.verywellmind.com/tapping-for-anxiety-how-it-works-and-how-to-do-it-7550116.

Wisneski, Len, and Lucy Anderson. "The Scientific Basis of Integrative Medicine." *Evidence-Based Complementary and Alternative Medicine* 2, no. 2 (June 2005): 257–59.

https://doi.org/10.1093/ecam/neh079.

Y. J. Editors. "Yoga Poses to Help You Balance Your Chakras." *Yoga Journal* (blog), March 14, 2023.

https://www.yogajournal.com/practice/yoga-sequences/7-poses-chakras/.